MOVIE ★ ICONS

DEAN

EDITOR
PAUL DUNCAN

TEXT
F. X. FEENEY

PHOTOS
THE KOBAL COLLECTION

TASCHEN

HONG KONG KÖLN LONDON LOS ANGELES MADRID PARIS TOKYO

CONTENTS

8
JAMES DEAN: SOUL REBEL

14 JAMES DEAN: REBELL MIT SEELE

18 JAMES DEAN: ÂME REBELLE

by F. X. Feeney

22
VISUAL FILMOGRAPHY

22 FILMOGRAFIE IN BILDERN

22 FILMOGRAPHIE EN IMAGES

180
CHRONOLOGY

184 CHRONOLOGIE

186 CHRONOLOGIE

188
FILMOGRAPHY

188 FILMOGRAFIE

188 FILMOGRAPHIE

192
BIBLIOGRAPHY

192 BIBLIOGRAFIE

192 BIBLIOGRAPHIE

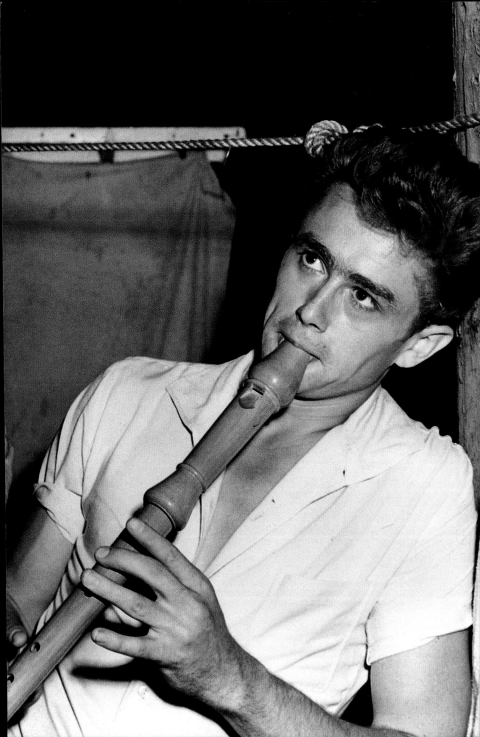

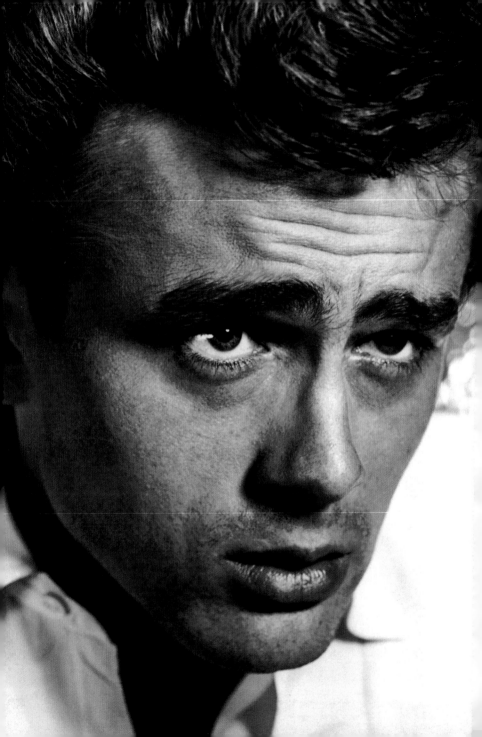

1

JAMES DEAN: SOUL REBEL

BY F. X. FEENEY

JAMES DEAN: REBELL MIT SEELE

JAMES DEAN : ÂME REBELLE

JAMES DEAN: SOUL REBEL

by F. X. Feeney

He died at age 24 in a car crash, testing a new, lightweight, ultra-swift Porsche Spyder en route to a weekend race in Northern California. The irony of ironies is that at the time he was driving safely within the speed limit. A distracted motorist in a much heavier car blindly ran a rural stop sign and James Dean was translated into a myth for the ages.

He excelled at playing rebels – yet in real life he was nowhere near as self-sabotaging as his hero Marlon Brando, nor as self-doomed as his other hero, Montgomery Clift. Dean was not so much reckless as he was fearless; a highly disciplined prodigy of ambition. Had chance favored him that evening, he might still be with us. He was six years younger than Paul Newman, roughly the same age as Clint Eastwood, Gene Hackman, Sean Connery, Peter O'Toole, Woody Allen, Dennis Hopper and Roman Polanski. He was not only passionately eager to act, but was carefully studying each of his directors as he rose through the ranks of television, theater and film, with an eye toward directing himself. Beyond the meteoric fame that greeted him from the first, a very great career beckoned.

Interesting to imagine what he might have done, given time. His plans after *Giant* included a performance as Hamlet on Broadway. We might thereafter have had a James Dean *Hud* (1963), a James Dean Virgil Hilts in *The Great Escape* (1963). Perhaps he would have rodeo-ridden the atom bomb in *Dr. Strangelove* (1964) instead of Slim Pickens, waving a cowboy hat and hollering for joy as the world ends. He would very likely have lost the lead in *The Godfather* (1972) to Brando no matter what (some roles are just fated), but then again one can easily picture him burning a hole in the screen with a shaved head as a much leaner, wilder Colonel Kurtz in *Apocalypse Now* (1979). Heaven knows, he might be even thriving to this day under the direction of Tim Burton, opposite his most direct spiritual offspring, Johnny Depp. Alas, none of this was to be – 'James Dean, Icon of Youth, Beauty & Genius' is what we

PORTRAIT FOR 'REBEL WITHOUT A CAUSE' (1955)

His air of defiance embodied the attitude of a generation. / Seine trotzige Ausstrahlung verkörperte die Haltung einer ganzen Generation. / Son air rebelle symbolise l'attitude de toute une génération.

"Dream as if you'll live forever, live as if you'll die today."
James Dean

have, and it survives in an immortal triple bill from the mid-1950s: *East of Eden* (1955), *Rebel Without a Cause* (1955) and *Giant* (1956).

Look at him, curled in an angry fetal position in the opening shots of the first two films. Seated atop a moving locomotive in *East of Eden*, he is fiercely, even a little comically oblivious to the spectacular north California scenery passing him – hopelessly locked into a fevered battle with his tyrannical father and a search for his long-lost mother. Dean's early life ran closely parallel to such pain – his mother died when he was eight years old, and his father coldly packed him off to live with Indiana relatives.

Prior to his emergence, teenagers in movies were uniformly clean-cut – role models, or monsters of bogus good cheer – but with his jazzy humor and unforced, unapologetic torment, Dean became something revolutionary, a spokesman, who could express with his whole body the rebellious anguish a generation of kids had been otherwise forbidden to articulate. In *Rebel Without a Cause* we find him not just curled fetally but flat on his face, dead drunk, laughing to himself as he prods a toy monkey at his fingertips. In the police station, he howls in loud mimicry of an approaching police siren – arguably the funniest and most self-mocking crybaby-whine in movies, then or thereafter. In *Giant*, under the direction of George Stevens (against whom Dean struggled in a tumultuous but fruitful battle of wills), he created a fascinating full-length portrait of a great American archetype – the dirt-poor cowboy who strikes it rich with an oil well and, with time, sours into a reclusive, ornery, Howard Hughes-like Rebel Against Himself.

What would James Dean have become, had he lived? Would he have cancelled himself out creatively, like his heroes Brando and Clift? Or would he have found a firm footing, and blazed a trail so great that even his most gifted rivals would gape in awe? Most of us would no doubt prefer to vote for the latter – but we can never truly know, and *that* is why he is forever so emblematic of gifted youth. Even 50 years after his death, we still look at James Dean in full suspense, wondering how he's going to turn out.

ENDPAPERS/VOR- UND NACHSATZBLÄTTER/
PAGES DE GARDE
STILL FROM 'GIANT' (1956)
James Dean as the eternal loner Jett Rink. / James Dean als ewiger Einzelgänger Jett Rink. / James Dean dans le rôle de Jett Rink, l'éternel solitaire.

PAGES 2/3
STILL FROM 'EAST OF EDEN' (1955)
As Cal Trask, desperately seeking the truth about his mother. / Als Cal Trask, der verzweifelt versucht, die Wahrheit über seine Mutter herauszufinden. / Dans le rôle de Cal Trask, recherchant désespérément la vérité sur sa mère.

PAGE 4
PORTRAIT FOR 'EAST OF EDEN' (1955)
Groomed for stardom. / Als Star herausgeputzt. / Graine de star.

PAGES 6/7
ON THE SET OF 'EAST OF EDEN' (1955)
Dean befriended costar Burl Ives (left) through music. / Über die Musik freundete sich Dean mit seinem Kollegen Burl Ives (links) an. / La musique le rapproche de son partenaire Burl Ives (à gauche).

PAGE 8
PORTRAIT FOR 'EAST OF EDEN' (1955)
A characteristic image of Dean's intense vulnerability. / Ein typisches Bild, das Deans tiefe Verletzlichkeit zeigt. / Image caractéristique de son intense vulnérabilité.

OPPOSITE/RECHTS/CI-CONTRE
PORTRAIT (1955)

JAMES DEAN: REBELL MIT SEELE

von F. X. Feeney

Er war 24, auf dem Weg zu einem Wochenendrennen in Nordkalifornien, als er in seinem neuen, sehr leichten und sehr schnellen Porsche Spyder bei einem Autounfall starb. Ironischerweise hielt er sich zum Zeitpunkt des Unglücks genau an die Geschwindigkeitsbegrenzung. Ein anderer Autofahrer in einem viel schwereren Fahrzeug hatte ein Stoppschild an der Landstraße missachtet, und so bescherte dieses Unglück künftigen Generationen den Mythos „James Dean".

Dean glänzte in der Rolle des jungen Rebellen – doch im Leben war er nicht annähernd so selbstzerstörerisch veranlagt wie sein Vorbild Marlon Brando oder durch eigenes Zutun zum Scheitern verurteilt wie sein anderes Vorbild Montgomery Clift. Dean war weniger waghalsig als einfach nur furchtlos. Er war ein hochdisziplinierter und ehrgeiziger Wunderknabe. Wäre an jenem Abend das Glück auf seiner Seite gewesen, lebte er noch heute. Er war sechs Jahre jünger als Paul Newman und ungefähr genauso alt wie Clint Eastwood, Gene Hackman, Sean Connery, Peter O'Toole, Woody Allen, Dennis Hopper und Roman Polanski. Er war nicht nur ein leidenschaftlicher Schauspieler, sondern er beobachtete auch jeden seiner Regisseure sehr sorgfältig, während er sich über Fernsehen, Theater und Film hocharbeitete, um vielleicht eines Tages einmal selbst Regie führen zu können. Ungeachtet seines kometenhaften Aufstiegs schien ihm eine große Karriere bevorzustehen.

Es ist interessant, sich vorzustellen, was er noch alles getan hätte, wenn ihm die Zeit dazu geblieben wäre. Unter anderem plante er, nach *Giganten* den Hamlet am Broadway zu spielen. Möglicherweise hätten wir danach einen James Dean als *Der Wildeste unter tausend* (1963) gesehen oder einen James Dean als Virgil Hilts in *Gesprengte Ketten* (1963). Vielleicht hätte er auch anstelle von Slim Pickens in *Dr. Seltsam oder Wie ich lernte, die Bombe zu lieben* (1964) die Atombombe geritten, seinen Cowboyhut geschwungen und das Ende der Welt mit Freudenschreien begrüßt. Er hätte wohl auf jeden Fall die Hauptrolle in *Der Pate* (1972) an Brando verloren (einige Rollen sind einfach Schicksal), aber andererseits kann man ihn sich gut mit glatt rasiertem Schädel als einen wesentlich schlankeren und wilderen Colonel Kurtz in *Apocalypse Now*

ON THE SET OF 'REBEL WITHOUT A CAUSE' (1955)
Director Nicholas Ray shrewdly encouraged Dean's creative input. / Regisseur Nicholas Ray ermutigte Dean geschickt zur kreativen Mitsprache. / Le cinéaste Nicholas Ray encourage habilement sa créativité.

„Träume, als lebtest du ewig – lebe, als stürbest du heute."
James Dean

(1979) vorstellen, der die Leinwand zum Glühen gebracht hätte. Wer weiß, ob er vielleicht nicht heute mit großem Erfolg unter der Regie von Tim Burton spielen würde – an der Seite seines echten geistigen Ziehsohns, Johnny Depp. Doch all dies sollte nicht sein. Uns bleibt allein James Dean, das Jugend- und Schönheitsidol, das Genie, verewigt in einem unsterblichen Dreierprogramm aus der Mitte der Fünfzigerjahre: *Jenseits von Eden* (1955), *... denn sie wissen nicht, was sie tun* (1955) und *Giganten* (1956).

Schauen Sie ihn sich an in den Eingangsszenen der ersten beiden Filme – eingerollt wie ein zorniger Fötus. In *Jenseits von Eden* sitzt er auf einem fahrenden Zug, und doch entgeht ihm auf beinahe komische Weise die eindrucksvolle Landschaft Nordkaliforniens, die an ihm vorüberzieht, weil ihn die Auseinandersetzung mit seinem tyrannischen Vater und die Suche nach seiner verschollenen Mutter geradezu fieberhaft beschäftigen. Dean konnte diesen Schmerz aus eigener Erfahrung gut nachempfinden: Seine Mutter starb, als er acht war, und sein Vater hatte ihn eiskalt zu den Verwandten nach Indiana geschickt.

Bis zu seinem Erscheinen waren Teenager in Filmen stets einheitlich brav und ordentlich – Vorbilder eben – oder von furchtbar aufgesetzt wirkender guter Laune. Dann kam Dean wie der Fürsprecher einer neuen Generation: Mit seinem frechen Witz und seinem unverhohlenen Seelenschmerz wirkte es geradezu revolutionär, wie er mit seinem ganzen Körper die trotzige Seelenqual ausdrücken konnte, die Jugendliche bislang nicht öffentlich zeigen und ausleben durften.

In *... denn sie wissen nicht, was sie tun* liegt er nicht nur wie ein Fötus eingerollt, sondern auch noch flach auf seinem Gesicht, sturzbetrunken vor sich hinkichernd, während er mit den Fingerspitzen einen Spielzeugaffen anstößt. Auf dem Polizeirevier heult er zur Sirene eines herannahenden Streifenwagens – möglicherweise bis zum heutigen Tag das lustigste und selbstironischste Kindergejaule der Filmgeschichte. In *Giganten*, unter der Regie von George Stevens (mit dem sich Dean stürmische, doch letztendlich fruchtbare Auseinandersetzungen lieferte), schuf er ein faszinierendes, abendfüllendes Porträt eines großen amerikanischen Archetyps: der bettelarme Cowboy, der auf Öl stößt, plötzlich reich wird und im Laufe der Zeit zu einem zurückgezogenen, übellaunigen Howard-Hughes-Typen versauert, der letztendlich gegen sich selbst rebelliert.

Was wäre aus James Dean geworden, wenn er überlebt hätte? Hätte er sich schöpferisch selbst im Weg gestanden wie seine Vorbilder Brando und Clift? Oder hätte er Fuß gefasst und ein Lebenswerk geschaffen, vor dem selbst seine talentiertesten Kollegen nur ehrfürchtig den Hut ziehen könnten? Die meisten von uns würden gerne an Letzteres glauben – aber wir werden es eben nie wissen. Und genau das macht ihn zum Emblem, zum Inbegriff des talentierten, genialen Jungen. Noch ein halbes Jahrhundert nach seinem Tod schauen wir gespannt zu James Dean auf und fragen uns, was wohl aus ihm einmal werden wird.

ON THE SET OF 'REBEL WITHOUT A CAUSE' (1955)
Ever delighting at the unexpected. / Dean freute sich immer über eine Überraschung. / Un goût prononcé pour l'inattendu.

JAMES DEAN : ÂME REBELLE

F. X. Feeney

James Dean est mort à 24 ans dans un accident de voiture, alors qu'il testait un nouveau bolide Porsche Spyder ultraléger en se rendant à une course automobile dans le nord de la Californie. Comble de l'ironie, il respectait scrupuleusement la limite de vitesse au moment de l'accident. Mais il suffit qu'un conducteur distrait au volant d'une grosse berline brûle un stop sur une route de campagne pour que James Dean accède au statut de mythe pour l'éternité.

S'il excellait dans les rôles de rebelles, il était loin, dans la vraie vie, de se montrer aussi autodestructeur que son idole, Marlon Brando, ni aussi suicidaire que son autre héros, Montgomery Clift. Dean n'était pas tant imprudent qu'intrépide ; sa prodigieuse ambition se doublait d'une discipline de fer. Si la chance lui avait souri ce soir-là, il serait peut-être encore parmi nous aujourd'hui. Né six ans après Paul Newman, il avait à peu près le même âge que Clint Eastwood, Gene Hackman, Sean Connery, Peter O'Toole, Woody Allen, Dennis Hopper et Roman Polanski. Bien qu'animé d'une ardente envie de jouer, il étudia minutieusement chacun de ses metteurs en scène à mesure qu'il gravissait les échelons de la télévision, du théâtre et du cinéma, dans l'espoir de passer un jour derrière la caméra. Au-delà du succès fulgurant qu'il connut dès ses débuts, une magnifique carrière l'attendait.

Difficile d'imaginer ce qu'il serait devenu avec le temps. Après *Géant*, il prévoyait notamment d'incarner Hamlet à Broadway. Il aurait ensuite pu interpréter *Le Plus Sauvage d'entre tous* (1963) ou Virgil Hilts dans *La Grande Évasion* (1963). Peut-être aurait-il chevauché la bombe atomique à la place de Slim Pickens dans *Dr Folamour* (1964), agitant son chapeau de cow-boy et hurlant de joie à l'approche de la fin du monde. Sans doute n'aurait-il pu ravir la vedette à Marlon Brando dans *Le Parrain* (1972) (certains rôles portent la marque du destin), mais on l'imagine fort bien capable de crever l'écran en campant un colonel Kurtz beaucoup plus maigre et farouche dans *Apocalypse Now* (1979). Qui sait s'il ne brillerait pas aujourd'hui encore sous la direction de Tim Burton aux côtés de son héritier spirituel le plus direct,

ON THE SET OF 'REBEL WITHOUT A CAUSE' (1955)
Flirting with a clearly besotted Natalie Wood. / Beim Flirt mit der sichtbar hingerissenen Natalie Wood. / Flirtant avec Natalie Wood, totalement entichée de lui.

« Rêve comme si tu devais vivre pour toujours, vis comme si tu devais mourir aujourd'hui. »
James Dean

Johnny Depp. Hélas, le sort en a décidé autrement. James Dean demeurera à jamais un symbole de jeunesse, de beauté et de génie, immortalisé par un trio de films inoubliables tournés au milieu des années 1950 : *À l'est d'Éden* (1955), *La Fureur de vivre* (1955) et *Géant* (1956).

James Dean, c'est cet adolescent recroquevillé comme un fœtus sous l'effet de la colère dans les séquences d'ouverture de ses deux premiers films. C'est ce jeune homme assis sur le toit d'un train en marche dans *À l'est d'Éden*, farouchement indifférent aux paysages spectaculaires qui défilent sous ses yeux. Enfermé dans un combat fébrile contre un père tyrannique et la quête désespérée d'une mère depuis longtemps disparue. Situation qui rappelle étrangement les premières années de la vie de l'acteur, qui perdit sa mère à l'âge de huit ans et que son père envoya froidement vivre chez sa tante, quelque part dans l'Indiana.

Avant James Dean, les personnages d'adolescents étaient uniformément stéréotypés : héros exemplaires ou monstres de bonne humeur factice. Mais avec son humour enjoué et son mal-être sincère et décomplexé, Dean devint une icône révolutionnaire, un porte-parole capable d'exprimer avec tout son être l'angoisse et la rébellion d'une génération jusque-là condamnée à les taire. Dans *La Fureur de vivre*, il apparaît non seulement en position fœtale, mais aussi ivre mort, allongé face contre terre ou accaparé par un singe en peluche. Dans la scène du commissariat, le hurlement geignard qu'il pousse en imitant une sirène de police reste dans la mémoire du cinéma comme un chef-d'œuvre d'humour et d'autodérision. Dans *Géant*, de George Stevens (à la volonté duquel il se heurte de façon aussi tumultueuse que féconde), il brosse longuement le portrait d'un grand archétype américain : celui du misérable cow-boy faisant fortune grâce au pétrole, mais qui devient avec le temps un personnage aigri, reclus et acariâtre à la Howard Hughes, en rébellion contre lui-même.

Que serait devenu James Dean s'il avait survécu ? Se serait-il brûlé les ailes comme ses idoles, Brando et Clift ? Ou aurait-il trouvé ses marques et effectué une trajectoire si phénoménale que même les plus doués de ses rivaux en seraient restés bouche bée ? Si beaucoup d'entre nous penchent probablement pour la seconde hypothèse, nul ne peut l'accréditer avec certitude, et c'est précisément pour cela qu'il demeure à jamais l'emblème de la jeunesse. Cinquante ans après sa mort, James Dean continue de nous captiver, comme si nous attendions de savoir ce qu'il va devenir.

PAGE 22
PORTRAIT (1933)
A presence to be reckoned with, even at age two. / Schon im Alter von zwei Jahren eine stattliche Persönlichkeit. / Une présence non négligeable, même à l'âge de deux ans.

PORTRAIT FOR 'EAST OF EDEN' (1955)
His embrace of Julie Harris has a suitably melancholy gravity. / Die melancholische Schwere, mit der er Julie Harris umarmt, passt zur Situation. / Son étreinte avec Julie Harris est empreinte d'une gravité mélancolique de circonstance.

2

VISUAL FILMOGRAPHY

FILMOGRAFIE IN BILDERN
FILMOGRAPHIE EN IMAGES

EARLY DAYS

FRÜHE JAHRE

LES JEUNES ANNÉES

PORTRAIT (1942)
Left to his own devices after his mother's death. / Nach dem Tod seiner Mutter war er ganz auf sich selbst gestellt. / Livré à lui-même après le décès de sa mère.

"Instead of doing little poems about mice, I did things like 'The Terror of Death' – the goriest. This made me strange – a little harpy in short pants."
James Dean on performing as a child at family gatherings

„Statt niedlicher Gedichte über Mäuse nahm ich mir Sachen wie ‚Der Schrecken des Todes' vor – richtig blutrünstiges Zeug. Dadurch wirkte ich etwas sonderbar – wie ein kleiner Blutsauger in kurzen Hosen."
James Dean über seine Auftritte als Kind bei Familienfeiern

PORTRAIT (1939)
A skilled charmer by age eight. His loving mother no doubt took this photo. / Mit acht war er bereits ein gewiefter Charmeur. Diese Aufnahme stammt mit Sicherheit von seiner Mutter, die ihn über alles liebte. / Charmeur invétéré dès huit ans, dans un cliché sans doute pris sous l'œil aimant de sa mère.

« Au lieu de réciter des petites histoires de souris, je déclamais des poèmes atroces comme La Terreur de la mort. Cela faisait de moi une sorte de harpie en culottes courtes. »
James Dean narrant les réunions de famille de son enfance

PORTRAIT (1946)
Dean (front row, center) mourned the loss of his mother but made friends and proved a good athlete. / Dean (vordere Reihe, Mitte) trauerte um seine Mutter, doch er fand Freunde und erbrachte gute Leistungen im Sport. / Malgré son drame familial, James (au centre, au premier rang) devient un adolescent sportif et sociable.

PORTRAIT (1953)
The 'iconic' Dean we now remember formed early. / Die ‚Ikone' Dean, an die wir uns heute noch erinnern, war schon sehr früh ausgeprägt. / L'image emblématique passée à la postérité apparaît assez tôt.

PAGES 28/29
STILL FROM 'THE UNLIGHTED ROAD' (1955)
A young drifter, tempted into a life of crime opposed by costar Pat Hardy. / Dean spielt an der Seite von Pat Hardy einen jungen Herumtreiber, der in kriminelle Versuchung gerät. / Un jeune homme à la dérive, tenté par la vie de hors-la-loi à laquelle s'oppose sa partenaire Pat Hardy.

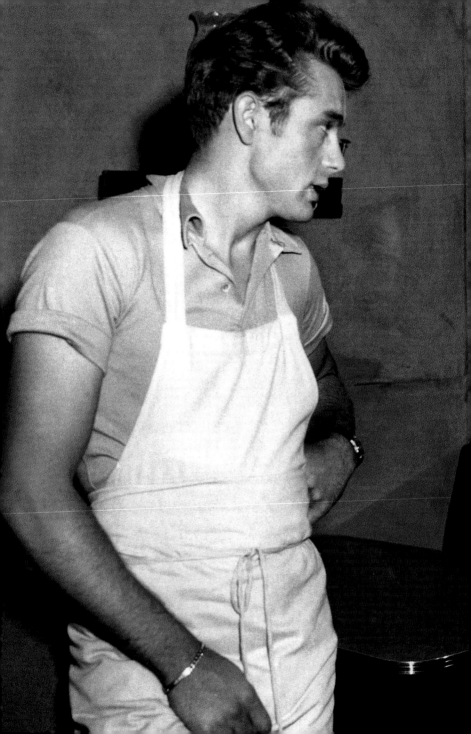

PORTRAIT FOR 'THE UNLIGHTED ROAD' (1955)
Leather jackets were a ready symbol of self-reliance in
the 1950s. They still are. / Lederjacken waren in den
1950er-Jahren ein Symbol des Selbstbewusstseins – und
sind es bis heute geblieben. / Des années 1950 à nos
jours, le blouson de cuir a toujours été un symbole
d'indépendance.

PORTRAIT FOR 'THE UNLIGHTED ROAD' (1955)
This minor-key TV drama boasts a fine performance by
Dean. / In diesem kleinen Fernsehspiel liefert Dean eine
solide darstellerische Leistung. / Belle prestation de
James Dean dans ce téléfilm en mode mineur.

PAGES 32 & 33
PORTRAITS (1955)
A trained dancer, he could easily adopt any manner,
head to toe. / Als ausgebildetem Tänzer fiel ihm
jede Körperhaltung leicht – vom Kopf bis zu den
Zehenspitzen. / Grâce à ses cours de danse, il sait
habiter de la tête au pied n'importe quel personnage.

"Acting is the most logical way for people's
neuroses to express themselves."
James Dean

„Die Schauspielerei ist die logischste Art und
Weise, in der sich die Neurosen der Menschen
ausdrücken können."
James Dean

« Être acteur est la meilleure façon d'exprimer
ses névroses. »
James Dean

RIGHT/RECHTS/CI-CONTRE
PORTRAIT (1955)
A future 007? No, this shot was a teaser for his role in
'East of Eden.' / James Dean – ein künftiger 007? Nein,
diese Aufnahme stammt aus der Ankündigung für seine
Rolle in *Jenseits von Eden*. / Un futur 007 ? Non, une
photo d'accroche pour son rôle dans *À l'est d'Éden*.

PAGES 36 & 37
PORTRAITS (1955)
At that time, every new face at Warner Bros. posed with
these sculpted horses. / Damals musste sich jeder
Neuling bei Warner Bros. mit dieser Pferdeskulptur
ablichten lassen. / À l'époque, toutes les nouvelles
recrues de la Warner Bros. posent avec ces statues de
chevaux.

PORTRAIT (1955)
He loved race cars, but was a careful, calculating driver.
By no means reckless. / Er liebte Rennwagen, aber er
war ein vorsichtiger und berechnender Fahrer und
keinesfalls waghalsig. / Malgré son goût pour les
voitures de course, Dean est un conducteur avisé
qui n'a rien d'un casse-cou.

PORTRAIT (1955)
Speed was in Dean's nature. Precision, too. /
Geschwindigkeit lag Dean ebenso im Blut wie
Genauigkeit. / La vitesse est dans sa nature.
La précision également.

PAGE 40
PORTRAIT FOR 'EAST OF EDEN' (1955)
With Julie Harris. / Mit Julie Harris. / Avec Julie Harris.

"I used to go out for the cows on a motorcycle.
Scared the hell out of them. They'd get to running
and their udders would start swinging, and they'd
lose a quart of milk."
James Dean

„Ich jagte auf meinem Motorrad Kühe. Sie waren
zu Tode erschreckt und rannten davon. Dabei
schwangen ihre Euter hin und her, und sie verloren
rund einen Liter Milch."
James Dean

« J'allais chercher les vaches en moto. Je leur
flanquais une peur bleue. Elles se mettaient à
courir, leurs pis se balançaient et elles perdaient
un litre de lait. »
James Dean

EAST OF EDEN

JENSEITS VON EDEN

À L'EST D'ÉDEN

STILL FROM 'EAST OF EDEN' (1955)
Details like this ancient, overturned boat give the story a mythical dimension. / Details wie dieses alte umgekippte Boot verleihen der Geschichte eine mythische Dimension. / Des détails comme ce vieux bateau renversé confèrent à l'histoire une dimension mythique.

STILL FROM 'EAST OF EDEN' (1955)
The silvery coastal light of Monterey sets the atmospheric stage for the hero's quest. / Das silbrige Licht an der Küste von Monterey schafft die passende Atmosphäre für die Suche des Protagonisten. / La lumière argentée de Monterey instaure une atmosphère particulière autour de la quête du héros.

PAGES 44/45
STILL FROM 'EAST OF EDEN' (1955)
Engaged in a primal quest – seeking the mother (Jo Van Fleet, right) he has never met. / Ein uraltes Motiv: die Suche nach der Mutter (Jo Van Fleet, rechts), die er nie gekannt hat. / Engagé dans une quête vitale, à la recherche d'une mère qu'il n'a pas connue (Jo Van Fleet, à droite).

STILL FROM 'EAST OF EDEN' (1955)
Afraid to face his mother, Cal returns to Salinas Valley
by rail. / Cal hat Angst davor, seiner Mutter
gegenüberzutreten, und fährt mit dem Zug zurück ins
Salinas-Tal. / N'osant affronter sa mère, Cal rentre en
train à Salinas Valley.

"You've got to live fast; death comes early."
James Dean

„Du musst schnell leben; der Tod kommt früh."
James Dean

« Il faut vivre vite ; la mort a tôt fait d'arriver. »
James Dean

STILL FROM 'EAST OF EDEN' (1955)
This shot was cut from the film, but it shows Dean's
physical exuberance. / Diese Einstellung wurde nicht im
Film verwendet, doch sie zeigt sehr gut Deans
körperliche Fitness. / Ce plan coupé au montage
montre l'exubérance physique de l'acteur.

STILL FROM 'EAST OF EDEN' (1955)
Cal and his brother Aron (Richard Davalos) both love
Abra (Julie Harris). / Cal und sein Bruder Aron (Richard
Davalos) lieben beide Abra (Julie Harris). / Cal et son
frère Aron (Richard Davalos), tous deux amoureux
d'Abra (Julie Harris).

'About the boy, James Dean, inasmuch as your
impression of him is a good one, we naturally will
go along with you. You said he is an odd kid. I hope
he isn't too odd as it's getting to the point now that
when we make pictures with odd people, the whole
machine is thrown out of order. You know it only
takes one odd spark plug to make the whole motor
miss.'
Jack Warner, memo to Elia Kazan, 10 March 1954

„Was den Jungen, James Dean, angeht und den
guten Eindruck, den Sie von ihm haben, so
schließen wir uns natürlich Ihrer Meinung an.
Sie sagten, er sei sonderbar. Ich hoffe nur, dass er
nicht wie andere Sonderlinge ist, mit denen wir
Filme gedreht haben und von denen die gesamte
Maschinerie durcheinandergeschüttelt wird. Sie
wissen ja: Schon eine einzige Fehlzündung kann
den ganzen Motor lahmlegen."
Jack Warner, Memorandum an Elia Kazan, 10. März 1954

STILL FROM 'EAST OF EDEN' (1955)
John Steinbeck's novel retold the Biblical story of Cain and Abel (i. e. Cal and Aron). However, director Elia Kazan deleted several scenes between the two brothers, such as this one. / John Steinbecks Roman war eine Nacherzählung der biblischen Geschichte von Kain und Abel (hier Cal und Aron). Regisseur Elia Kazan schnitt aber mehrere Szenen wie diese mit den beiden Brüdern. / Bien que le roman de John Steinbeck retrace l'histoire biblique d'Abel et Caïn (Aron et Cal), le réalisateur Elia Kazan supprime plusieurs scènes entre les deux frères, dont celle-ci.

PAGES 50/51
STILL FROM 'EAST OF EDEN' (1955)
Cal unleashes his rage at the world, unaware he is being watched. / Cal lässt seinem Zorn über die Welt freien Lauf und bemerkt nicht, dass er dabei beobachtet wird. / Ne se sachant pas observé, Cal laisse éclater sa rage contre le monde.

« En ce qui concerne le jeune James Dean, dans la mesure où il vous fait bonne impression, nous nous rangerons naturellement à votre avis. Vous avez dit que c'est un gamin bizarre. J'espère qu'il ne l'est pas trop, car maintenant, quand nous tournons avec des gens bizarres, toute la machine tombe en panne. Vous savez qu'il suffit d'une seule bougie défectueuse pour que le moteur ait des ratés. »
Jack Warner, note à Elia Kazan, 10 mars 1954

COSTUME DEPT. PROD. 810
NAME JAMES DEAN
PART CAL TRASK
CHG.# 2 SC. 51-66
EXT. RAILROAD YARD

STILL FROM 'EAST OF EDEN' (1955)
Cal's deeper quest is to win approval from his father
(Raymond Massey). / Cals eigentliches Ziel ist die
Anerkennung durch seinen Vater (Raymond Massey). /
Le véritable objet de sa quête est en fait l'approbation
de son père (Raymond Massey).

ON THE SET OF 'EAST OF EDEN' (1955)
Dean, raised on a farm, quite naturally rests his hands
between the straps in this costume test. / Für Dean, der
auf einem Bauernhof aufwuchs, war es ganz normal, die
Hände bei dieser Kostümprobe hinter die Hosenträger
zu stecken. / Ayant grandi dans une ferme, James Dean
se cale tout naturellement les mains dans les bretelles
de sa salopette lors de cet essai de costume.

STILL FROM 'EAST OF EDEN' (1955)
Abra may admire Aron but she loves the moody Cal. /
Wenngleich Abra Aron bewundert, liebt sie doch den
launischen Cal. / Malgré son admiration pour Aron, c'est
de Cal le ténébreux qu'Abra est amoureuse.

*"When he walked into the office, I knew he was
right for the role. He was guarded, sullen,
suspicious, and he seemed to me to have a great
deal of concealed emotion. He looked and spoke
like the character in 'East of Eden.'"*
Elia Kazan, 30 September 1985

STILL FROM 'EAST OF EDEN' (1955)
Director Elia Kazan recalled that Dean was fascinated by Harris and she anchored him. / Regisseur Elia Kazan erinnerte sich, dass Dean von Harris sehr angetan war und sie ihm Halt gab. / Selon le réalisateur Elia Kazan, Dean était fasciné par Julie Harris, qui le stabilisait.

„Als er ins Büro kam, wusste ich, dass er der Richtige war für die Rolle. Er war zurückhaltend, mürrisch, misstrauisch, und er schien mir eine ganze Menge an Gefühlen zu verbergen. Er sah aus und sprach wie die Figur in Jenseits von Eden."
Elia Kazan, 30. September 1985

« Quand il est entré dans le bureau, j'ai tout de suite su qu'il était fait pour le rôle. Il était sur ses gardes, maussade, méfiant, et il m'a semblé cacher beaucoup d'émotions. Il avait tout du personnage d'À l'est d'Éden. »
Elia Kazan, 30 septembre 1985

STILL FROM 'EAST OF EDEN' (1955)
Cal discovers his mother owns a brothel. Lois Smith
(left) works there: Are she and Cal related? / Cal findet
heraus, dass seine Mutter ein Bordell besitzt. Anne
(Lois Smith, links) arbeitet dort: Ist sie etwa mit Cal
verwandt? / Cal découvre que sa mère tient un bordel.
Lois Smith (à gauche) et le jeune homme sont-ils
parents ?

*"I'm a serious-minded and intense little devil –
terribly gauche and so tense that I don't see how
people can stay in the same room as me. I know
I couldn't tolerate myself."*
James Dean

*„Ich bin ein ernsthafter und konzentrierter kleiner
Teufel – unheimlich linkisch und so angespannt,
dass ich nicht verstehen kann, wie es Menschen in
einem Raum mit mir aushalten. Ich weiß, ich könnte
es nicht."*
James Dean

STILL FROM 'EAST OF EDEN' (1955)
Cal's mother (Jo Van Fleet) faces him for the first
time. / Cals Mutter (Jo Van Fleet) begegnet ihm zum
ersten Mal wieder. / Cal se retrouve pour la première
fois face à sa mère (Jo Van Fleet).

*« Je suis un affreux gamin qui prend tout très au
sérieux. Je suis atrocement gauche et tellement
tendu que je ne comprends pas comment les gens
peuvent rester dans la même pièce que moi.
Personnellement, je n'arriverais pas à me
supporter. »*
James Dean

"I can't divert into being a social human being when I'm working on a hero like Cal, who's essentially demonic."
James Dean

„Ich kann mich nicht plötzlich in einen geselligen Menschen verwandeln, wenn ich an einem Protagonisten wie Cal arbeite, der im Grunde ein Dämon ist."
James Dean

« Je ne peux pas redevenir un être humain sociable quand je travaille sur un personnage comme Cal, qui est fondamentalement démoniaque. »
James Dean

STILL FROM 'EAST OF EDEN' (1955)
Timothy Carey plays the ogre at the gates, guarding Cal's mother. / Timothy Carey spielt den Türsteher, der Cals Mutter bewacht. / Timothy Carey incarne l'ogre qui protège la mère de Cal.

PAGES 60/61
PORTRAIT FOR 'EAST OF EDEN' (1955)
To make money for his father, and to show his worth, Cal invests in beans and profits from World War One. / Um für seinen Vater Geld zu beschaffen und ihm zu beweisen, was in ihm steckt, investiert Cal in Bohnen und profitiert vom Ersten Weltkrieg. / Pour rapporter de l'argent à son père et prouver sa valeur, Cal investit dans les haricots et profite de la Première Guerre mondiale.

ON THE SET OF 'EAST OF EDEN' (1955)
Dean was an infamous, amorous free spirit, but fell
passionately in love with actress Pier Angeli. / Dean war
in der Liebe ein berüchtigter Freigeist, doch in seine
Schauspielkollegin Pier Angeli hatte er sich
leidenschaftlich verliebt. / Bien que notoirement
volage, James Dean tombe passionnément amoureux
de l'actrice Pier Angeli.

*"Just an easy kind of friendly thing. I respect her.
She's untouchable. We're members of totally
different castes. You know, she's the kind of girl you
put on a shelf and look at. Anyway her old lady
[her mother] doesn't like me. Can't say I blame her."*
James Dean, on dating actress Pier Angeli

*„Das ist nur eine ganz lockere Freundschaft. Ich
respektiere sie. Sie ist unnahbar. Wir gehören zwei
völlig unterschiedlichen Kasten an. Wissen Sie, sie
ist die Art von Frau, die man ins Regal stellt und
anschaut. Wie dem auch sei, ihre Alte [ihre Mutter]
mag mich nicht. Und das kann ich ihr nicht
verübeln."*
**James Dean über seine Beziehung zu seiner
Schauspielkollegin Pier Angeli**

ON THE SET OF 'EAST OF EDEN' (1955)

Angeli's father forced her to marry someone else. Dean loudly revved his motorcycle outside the church, in protest. / Angelis Vater zwang sie, jemand anderen zu heiraten. Aus Protest ließ Dean vor der Kirche sein Motorrad laut aufheulen. / Le jour où le père de Pier Angeli la force à en épouser un autre, Dean fait vrombir sa moto sur le parvis de l'église en signe de protestation.

« C'est juste un lien amical. Je la respecte. Elle est intouchable. Nous appartenons à des castes totalement différentes. Vous savez, c'est le genre de fille qu'on pose sur une étagère pour la regarder. De toute façon, sa vieille [sa mère] ne m'aime pas. Je la comprends. »
James Dean au sujet de ses relations avec l'actrice Pier Angeli

ON THE SET OF 'EAST OF EDEN' (1955)
Between takes with Davalos, Harris, Harold Gordon and
a flirty Lois Smith. / Zwischen den Aufnahmen mit
Davalos, Harris, Harold Gordon und einer koketten Lois
Smith. / Entre deux prises avec Richard Davalos, Julie
Harris, Harold Gordon et une Lois Smith enjôleuse.

"No one ever did anything for me. I don't owe
anything to anyone."
James Dean

„Niemand hat jemals etwas für mich getan.
Ich schulde niemandem irgendetwas."
James Dean

« Personne n'a jamais rien fait pour moi. Je ne dois
rien à personne. »
James Dean

STILL FROM 'EAST OF EDEN' (1955)
War looms: Abra is a nurse; Aron, a conscientious
objector; Cal, an amateur profiteer. / Der Krieg
droht: Abra ist Krankenschwester, Aron
Kriegsdienstverweigerer und Cal ein nebenberuflicher
Kriegsgewinnler. / Lorsque survient la guerre, Abra
devient infirmière, Aron objecteur de conscience et Cal
simple profiteur.

STILL FROM 'EAST OF EDEN' (1955)
An accidental encounter at a fair sparks romance
between Abra and Cal. / Bei einer zufälligen Begegnung
auf dem Jahrmarkt springt der Funke über zwischen
Abra and Cal. / Leur rencontre inopinée dans une fête
foraine fait jaillir une étincelle entre Abra et Cal.

STILL FROM 'EAST OF EDEN' (1955)
Laughing and comfortable together in the funhouse
mirrors. / Im Spiegelkabinett haben die beiden Spaß
und fühlen sich wohl. / Moment de rire et de complicité
au milieu des miroirs déformants.

ON THE SET OF 'EAST OF EDEN' (1955)
Marlon Brando visits director Elia Kazan (left) on the
set. Dean pretends to be indifferent. / Marlon Brando
besucht Regisseur Elia Kazan (links) bei den
Dreharbeiten. Dean gibt sich gleichgültig. / Marlon
Brando rend visite à Elia Kazan (à gauche) sur le
tournage. James Dean feint l'indifférence.

"People were telling me I behaved like Brando
even before I knew who Brando was. I'm not
disturbed by the comparison – nor am I flattered."
James Dean

„Die Leute sagten mir schon, ich führte mich wie
Brando auf, bevor ich überhaupt wusste, wer
Brando war. Mich stört der Vergleich nicht – aber
ich fühle mich dadurch auch nicht geschmeichelt."
James Dean

STILL FROM 'EAST OF EDEN' (1955)
More funhouse fun, though deleted from the final
picture. / Noch mehr Spaß auf dem Jahrmarkt, der
allerdings der Schere zum Opfer fiel. / Une autre scène
cocasse, supprimée au montage.

« On me disait que je me comportais comme
Brando avant même que je sache qui c'était. La
comparaison ne me dérange pas, mais elle ne me
flatte pas non plus. »
James Dean

STILL FROM 'EAST OF EDEN' (1955)
The peace-loving Aron defends a German immigrant
from the mob, so Cal comes to his aid. / Der
friedliebende Aron verteidigt einen deutschen
Einwanderer, der vom Pöbel angegriffen wird, und
Cal kommt ihm zur Hilfe. / Lorsque Aron le pacifiste
défend un immigrant allemand agressé par la foule,
Cal arrive à la rescousse.

*"An actor must learn all there is to know,
experience all there is to experience, or approach
that state as closely as possible."*
James Dean

*„Ein Schauspieler muss alles lernen, was es zu
lernen gibt, alles erleben, was es zu erleben gibt,
oder wenigstens diesem Zustand so nahe wie
möglich kommen."*
James Dean

*« Un acteur doit apprendre tout ce qu'il faut savoir,
vivre tout ce qu'il faut avoir vécu, ou s'approcher le
plus possible de cet état. »*
James Dean

STILL FROM 'EAST OF EDEN' (1955)
Aron then learns about Abra's interest in Cal: an
explosion ensues. / Dann erfährt Aron, dass sich Abra
für Cal interessiert: Es kommt zu Handgreiflichkeiten. /
Mais quand Aron découvre les sentiments d'Abra pour
Cal, la confrontation est inévitable.

"I try so hard to make people reject me. Why?"
James Dean

„Ich arbeite so hart daran, Leute abzuschrecken.
Warum bloß?"
James Dean

« Je fais tout ce que je peux pour me faire rejeter.
Pourquoi ? »
James Dean

STILL FROM 'EAST OF EDEN' (1955)
The aftermath of the fight. / Nach der
Auseinandersetzung. / Après la bagarre.

STILL FROM 'EAST OF EDEN' (1955)
Cal visits Abra to plan his father's birthday party, and
decides to give his profits to his father, to pay the old
man's debts. / Cal besucht Abra, um die
Geburtstagsfeier für seinen Vater vorzubereiten.
Er entschließt sich, seine Gewinne dem Vater zu
schenken, damit dieser seine Schulden abbezahlen
kann. / Cal rend visite à Abra pour préparer
l'anniversaire de son père et décide de lui offrir
ses bénéfices pour éponger ses dettes.

"When you know there is something more to go in
a character, and you're not sure what it is, you just
got to go out after it. Walk on a tightrope."
James Dean to Dennis Hopper

„Wenn du weißt, dass in einer Figur noch mehr
steckt, und du dir nicht sicher bist, was es ist, dann
musst du einfach danach suchen. Es ist ein
Drahtseilakt."
James Dean zu Dennis Hopper

« Quand on sait qu'un personnage peut nous
emmener plus loin, mais qu'on ne sait pas vraiment
où, il faut s'engager à l'aveuglette. Marcher sur la
corde raide. »
James Dean à Dennis Hopper

ON THE SET OF 'EAST OF EDEN' (1955)
This is a rehearsal for the scene at left – note the
change in dress. / Eine Probe für die Szene links – man
beachte die unterschiedlichen Kostüme. / Répétition de
la scène de gauche ; notez le changement vestimentaire.

STILL FROM 'EAST OF EDEN' (1955)
If Cal is Cain from 'Genesis,' then his mother is Lilith,
Adam's sexy runaway bride, traditionally written out of
the Bible in favor of her successor, Eve. Here Cal asks
his mother's help in settling his father's debts. / Wenn
Cal Kain aus der Genesis entspricht, dann ist seine
Mutter Adams flüchtige Braut Lilith, die in der Bibel
traditionell zugunsten ihrer Nachfolgerin Eva
unterschlagen wird. Hier bittet Cal seine Mutter um
Hilfe bei der Tilgung der Schulden seines Vaters. / Si
Cal est le personnage de Caïn dans la Genèse, alors sa
mère est Lilith, la première compagne d'Adam, créature
lascive traditionnellement évincée de la Bible au profit
d'Ève, sa remplaçante. Cal demande ici l'aide de sa
mère pour éponger les dettes de son père.

"Don't 'act.' If you're smoking a cigarette, smoke it.
Don't act like you're smoking it."
James Dean to Dennis Hopper

„Tu nie so ‚als ob'. Wenn du eine Zigarette rauchst,
dann rauche sie. Tu nicht so, ‚als ob' du eine
Zigarette rauchst."
James Dean zu Dennis Hopper

« Il ne faut pas "jouer la comédie". Si tu fumes une
cigarette, fume-la. Ne joue pas l'homme en train de
fumer. »
James Dean to Dennis Hopper

"My purpose in life does not include a hankering to charm society."
James Dean

„Zum Sinn meines Lebens gehört nicht das Verlangen, mich der Gesellschaft anzubiedern."
James Dean

« Mon but dans la vie n'est pas de charmer la bonne société. »
James Dean

STILL FROM 'EAST OF EDEN' (1955)
Cal's father, Adam, openly prefers the other brother and waits for him, despite Cal having made all the party preparations. / Cals Vater Adam bevorzugt ganz offen den anderen Bruder und wartet auf ihn, obwohl Cal alle Vorbereitungen für die Feier getroffen hat. / Bien que Cal ait fait tous les préparatifs, son père attend manifestement son préféré, Aron.

STILL FROM 'EAST OF EDEN' (1955)
Adam angrily refuses Cal's help, despising any profit
made from the war. / Adam weist Cals Angebot wütend
zurück, weil er jeglichen Kriegsgewinn verabscheut. /
Méprisant les profits réalisés pendant la guerre, le père
refuse l'aide de son fils.

STILL FROM 'EAST OF EDEN' (1955)
Cal is devastated. / Cal ist am Boden zerstört. /
Le jeune homme s'effondre.

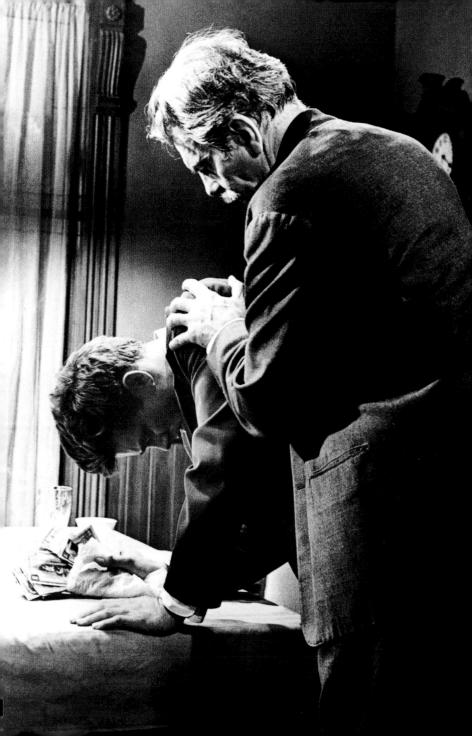

"I don't even want to be 'the best.' I want to grow so tall that nobody can reach me. Not to prove anything, but just to go where you ought to go when you devote your whole life and all you are to one thing."
James Dean

„Ich will nicht einfach ‚der Beste' sein. Sondern ich will so groß werden, dass niemand an mich heranreicht. Nicht, um irgendetwas zu beweisen, sondern nur, um dorthin zu gelangen, wohin man streben sollte, wenn man sein ganzes Leben und sein gesamtes Sein einem einzigen Ziel verschreibt."
James Dean

« Je ne veux même pas être "le meilleur". Je veux devenir tellement grand que personne ne pourra plus m'atteindre. Je ne veux rien prouver, je veux juste me retrouver à la place qu'on mérite quand on se consacre corps et âme à une seule chose. »
James Dean

STILL FROM 'EAST OF EDEN' (1955)
Cal takes his brother to their mother's whorehouse. Lois Smith cries out in this deleted scene. / Cal bringt seinen Bruder zum Freudenhaus ihrer Mutter. Lois Smith schreit nach ihm in dieser herausgeschnittenen Szene. / Cal emmène son frère au bordel de leur mère. Cette scène où Lois Smith l'interpelle a été coupée au montage.

"Whatever's inside making me what I am, it's like film. Film only works in the dark. Tear it all open and let in the light and you kill it."
James Dean

„Was auch in mir stecken mag und mich zu dem macht, was ich bin: Es ist wie Film. Film funktioniert auch nur im Dunkeln. Wenn man eine Filmpackung aufreißt und Licht hineinlässt, dann macht man den Film kaputt."
James Dean

« Ce qui est enfoui et qui fait de moi ce que je suis, c'est comme la pellicule. Ça ne marche que dans le noir. Si vous forcez la boîte et si vous laissez entrer la lumière, vous allez tout perdre. »
James Dean

STILL FROM 'EAST OF EDEN' (1955)
Aron goes hopelessly off to war. Adam suffers a stroke. Cal and Abra vow to care for him. / Ohne Hoffnung zieht Aron in den Krieg. Adam erleidet einen Schlaganfall. Cal und Abra geloben, sich um ihn zu kümmern. / Lorsque Aron se résigne à partir à la guerre, son père a une attaque ; Cal et Abra jurent de s'occuper de lui.

PAGE 86
STILL FROM 'REBEL WITHOUT A CAUSE' (1955)
Jim Stark (James Dean) vents his anger at his parents as the story opens in a police station. / Zu Beginn der Handlung macht Jim Stark (James Dean) auf dem Polizeirevier seiner Wut über die Eltern Luft. / Lorsque l'histoire débute au poste de police, Jim Stark (James Dean) déverse sa colère sur ses parents.

REBEL WITHOUT A CAUSE

... DENN SIE WISSEN NICHT, WAS SIE TUN

LA FUREUR DE VIVRE

STILL FROM 'REBEL WITHOUT A CAUSE' (1955)
Jim offers fellow delinquent Plato (Sal Mineo) his jacket, while troubled Judy (Natalie Wood) looks on. / Jim bietet dem frierenden Jugendstraftäter ,Plato' (Sal Mineo) seine Jacke an, während eine besorgte Judy (Natalie Wood) zuschaut. / Jim tend sa veste à Platon (Sal Mineo), son compagnon d'infortune, sous le regard troublé de Judy (Natalie Wood).

ON THE SET OF 'REBEL WITHOUT A CAUSE' (1955)
In the opening credits, a drunken Jim Stark covers the reclining toy monkey. Dean improvised the scene, which echoes Plato's death at the end. / In der Vorspannsequenz deckt der betrunkene Jim Stark den umgefallenen Spielzeugaffen zu. Dean improvisierte diese Szene, die „Platos" Tod am Ende des Films vorwegnimmt. / Dans le générique d'ouverture, Jim Stark, complètement ivre, joue avec un singe en peluche. Cette scène, improvisée par Dean, fait écho à la mort de Platon à la fin.

PAGES 90/91
STILL FROM 'REBEL WITHOUT A CAUSE' (1955)
Jim is outraged at the habitual hypocrisy of his Dad (Jim Backus). / Jim empört die notorische Scheinheiligkeit seines Vaters (Jim Backus). / Jim est outré par l'éternelle hypocrisie de son père (Jim Backus).

"Live fast, die young, and have a good-looking corpse."
Jim Stark, 'Rebel Without a Cause'

„Leb schnell, stirb jung und hinterlasse eine gut aussehende Leiche."
Jim Stark, ... denn sie wissen nicht, was sie tun

« Vivez vite, mourez jeune et faites un beau cadavre. »
Jim Stark, La Fureur de vivre

ON THE SET OF 'REBEL WITHOUT A CAUSE' (1955)
Director Nicholas Ray (right, hands on hips) coaches Natalie Wood (center) in her first serious adult role. /
Regisseur Nicholas Ray (rechts, mit den Händen an den Hüften) gibt Natalie Wood (Mitte) in ihrer ersten ernsthaften Erwachsenenrolle Hilfestellung. /
Le réalisateur Nicholas Ray (à droite, les mains sur les hanches) guide Natalie Wood (au centre) dans son premier vrai rôle d'adulte.

94

"I went out and hung around with kids in Los
Angeles before making 'Rebel Without a Cause.'
They wear leather jackets, go out looking for
someone to rough up a little. These aren't poor
kids, you know. Lots of them have money, grow up
and become pillars of the community. Boy, they
scared me!"
James Dean

„Ich ging raus und trieb mich mit Jugendlichen in
Los Angeles rum, bevor ich ... denn sie wissen
nicht, was sie tun drehte. Die tragen Lederjacken
und suchen nach Leuten, die sie ein wenig in die
Mangel nehmen können. Weißt du, das sind
keine armen Kinder. Viele von denen haben Geld,
und wenn sie groß sind, werden sie zu Stützen
der Gesellschaft. Junge, die haben mir Angst
eingejagt!"
James Dean

« Avant de tourner La Fureur de vivre, je suis allé
traîner avec des gosses de Los Angeles. Ils portent
des blousons de cuir et arpentent les rues en
cherchant la bagarre. Ce ne sont pas des gamins
déshérités, vous savez. Beaucoup d'entre eux ont
de l'argent, et une fois adultes, ils deviennent des
piliers de la société. Franchement, ils m'ont fait
peur ! »
James Dean

ON THE SET OF 'REBEL WITHOUT A CAUSE'
(1955)
This is first major American film to loudly proclaim that
school is hell. / Es war der erste große amerikanische
Film, der lautstark erklärte, dass Schule die Hölle sein
kann. / C'est le premier grand film américain à
proclamer haut et fort que l'école est un enfer.

**STILL FROM 'REBEL WITHOUT A CAUSE'
(1955)**
A deleted scene by the trophy cases, from Jim's first day at school. / Eine nicht verwendete Szene, in der Jim an seinem ersten Schultag an der Vitrine mit den Trophäen vorbeiläuft. / Scène coupée au montage, où Jim observe les trophées lors de sa première journée au lycée.

PAGES 98/99
**STILL FROM 'REBEL WITHOUT A CAUSE'
(1955)**
A friendship is born, onscreen and in life: with Sal Mineo (left) at Griffith Observatory. / Der Beginn einer Freundschaft – im Leben und auf der Leinwand: mit Sal Mineo (links) an der Griffith-Sternwarte. / Naissance d'une amitié à la ville comme à l'écran : avec Sal Mineo (à gauche) à l'observatoire Griffith.

**ON THE SET OF 'REBEL WITHOUT A CAUSE'
(1955)**
Conferring with director Nicholas Ray on the school steps. / Auf der Treppe des Schulgebäudes berät er sich mit Regisseur Nicholas Ray. / Conciliabule avec le réalisateur Nicholas Ray sur les marches du lycée.

**STILL FROM 'REBEL WITHOUT A CAUSE'
(1955)**
The gang, led by Buzz (Corey Allen, left), provoke Jim.
The real-life gang leader was Frank Mazzola (center),
who advised the production. Note Dennis Hopper (top
left). / Die Bande, die von Buzz (Corey Allen, links)
angeführt wird, provoziert Jim. Im wahren Leben war
Frank Mazzola (Mitte), der dem Film als Berater zur
Verfügung stand, der Boss der Bande. Man beachte
Dennis Hopper (oben links). / La bande de Buzz (Corey
Allen, à gauche) cherche à provoquer Jim. L'équipe suit
les conseils d'un ancien chef de bande, Frank Mazzola
(au centre). Noter la présence de Dennis Hopper (en
haut à gauche).

STILL FROM 'REBEL WITHOUT A CAUSE' (1955)
The provocation rapidly escalates into a knife fight. / Die Provokation eskaliert schnell zu einer Messerstecherei. / La provocation aboutit rapidement à un combat au couteau.

"What the hell are you doing? Can't you see I'm having a real moment? Don't you ever cut a scene when I'm having a real moment!"
James Dean on set to director Nicholas Ray

„*Was zum Teufel machen Sie? Sehen Sie nicht, dass ich gerade eine echte Eingebung habe? Unterbrechen Sie niemals eine Szene, wenn ich eine echte Eingebung habe!*"
James Dean am Set zu Regisseur Nicholas Ray

« *Qu'est-ce que tu fous, bon sang ? Tu ne vois pas que c'était un moment de vérité ? Ne coupe jamais une scène au milieu d'un moment de vérité !* »
James Dean au réalisateur Nicholas Ray

"He died at just the right time. If he had lived, he'd never have been able to live up to his publicity."
Humphrey Bogart

„Er starb gerade zur rechten Zeit. Wenn er am Leben geblieben wäre, hätte er dem Werberummel um seine Person niemals gerecht werden können."
Humphrey Bogart

« Il est mort juste au bon moment. S'il avait survécu, il n'aurait jamais pu être à la hauteur de sa réputation. »
Humphrey Bogart

STILL FROM 'REBEL WITHOUT A CAUSE' (1955)
The new boy in class proves to be no pushover. /
Der Neue lässt sich nicht so leicht unterkriegen. /
Le nouveau de la classe n'est pas du genre à se laisser faire.

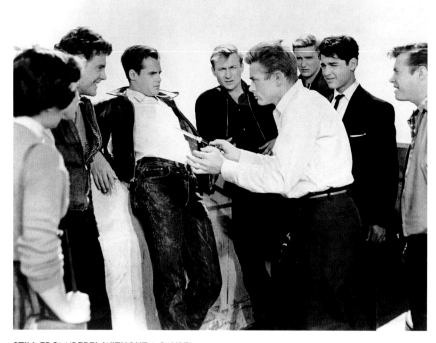

STILL FROM 'REBEL WITHOUT A CAUSE'
(1955)
Jim wins, only to be challenged to a deadlier ordeal –
a "chickie run." / Jim gewinnt den Kampf und wird zu
einem noch tödlicheren herausgefordert: einem
„Chickie Run" (in der deutschen Synchronfassung:
„Hasenfußrennen"). / La victoire de Jim lui vaudra un
défi encore plus périlleux, une course en voiture en
direction d'une falaise.

ON THE SET OF 'REBEL WITHOUT A CAUSE'
(1955)
Touching up a knife wound. / Eine ‚Stichwunde' wird
aufgebracht. / Retouche d'un coup de couteau.

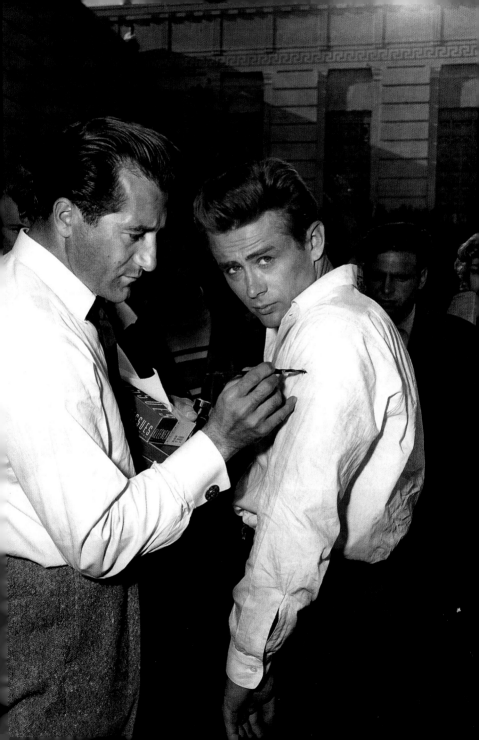

STILL FROM 'REBEL WITHOUT A CAUSE'
(1955)
Jim's aproned Dad means well, but is weak. / Jims Vater -
in der Schürze - hat gute Absichten, doch kann er sie
nicht verwirklichen. / Malgré ses bonnes intentions, le
père de Jim manque d'autorité.

"He prepared himself so well ... that the lines were
not simply something he'd memorized - they were
actually a very real part of him."
Jim Backus

„Er hat sich immer so gut vorbereitet ... Er hat seine
Texte nicht einfach nur auswendig gelernt - er hat
sie wirklich verinnerlicht."
Jim Backus

« Il se préparait tellement bien ... que les répliques
n'étaient pas seulement mémorisées, elles faisaient
partie intégrante de lui. »
Jim Backus

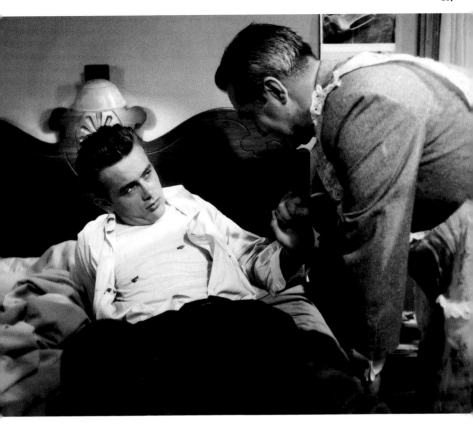

**STILL FROM 'REBEL WITHOUT A CAUSE'
(1955)**
There is love between father and son, but sadness and
anger too because Jim's father will not stand up for
himself. / Vater und Sohn mögen sich, doch Jim ist
wütend und traurig, weil sich sein Vater nicht
durchsetzen kann. / L'amour qui les unit est teinté de
tristesse et de colère, car son père ne sait pas s'affirmer.

**STILL FROM 'REBEL WITHOUT A CAUSE'
(1955)**
Jim and Buzz are on the verge of friendship before their
deadly race. / Vor ihrem tödlichen Wettrennen werden
Jim und Buzz beinahe zu Freunden. / Avant leur course
fatale, Jim et Buzz sont sur le point de se lier d'amitié.

*"I have never seen an actor as dedicated, with the
extreme concentration and exceptional
imagination, as James Dean."*
Dennis Hopper

*„Ich habe nie einen Schauspieler gesehen, der
so in seiner Arbeit aufging wie James Dean mit
seiner äußersten Konzentration und seiner
außergewöhnlichen Vorstellungskraft."*
Dennis Hopper

*« Je n'ai jamais vu un acteur aussi dévoué, avec une
concentration aussi extrême et une imagination
aussi exceptionnelle que James Dean. »*
Dennis Hopper

STILL FROM 'REBEL WITHOUT A CAUSE' (1955)
Judy wishes Jim luck with a handful of dirt. / Mit einer Handvoll Dreck (in der deutschen Synchronfassung „Sand") wünscht Judy Jim Glück. / Judy souhaite bonne chance à Jim avec une poignée de terre.

PAGES 110/111
STILL FROM 'REBEL WITHOUT A CAUSE' (1955)
In agony after Buzz is accidentallly killed in the "chicken run." / Der Unfalltod von Buzz beim Rennen geht Jim nicht aus dem Kopf. / Moment de détresse après la mort accidentelle de Buzz lors de la course en voiture.

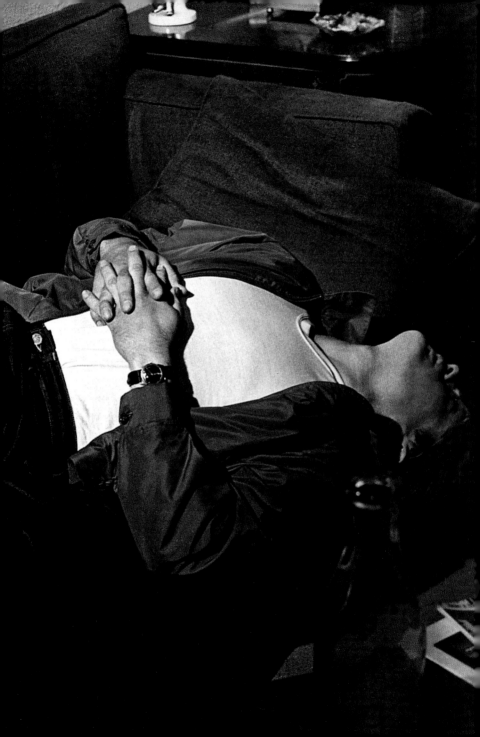

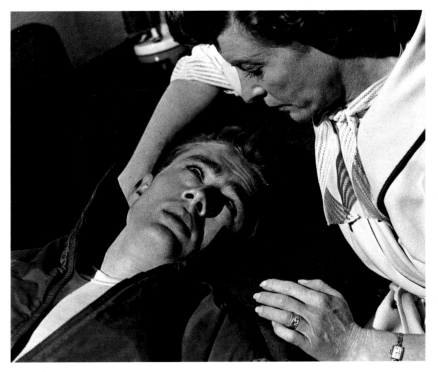

STILL FROM 'REBEL WITHOUT A CAUSE' (1955)
Jim wants to report his role in Buzz's death to the police, but his mother forbids him. / Jim möchte sich der Polizei stellen und erklären, welche Rolle er beim Tod von Buzz spielte, doch seine Mutter verbietet es ihm. / Jim veut avouer à la police son rôle dans la mort de Buzz, mais sa mère le lui interdit.

ON THE SET OF 'REBEL WITHOUT A CAUSE' (1955)
After rehearsing at Nicholas Ray's house, his stairs were recreated in the studio. / Nach einem Probedurchlauf im Haus von Nicholas Ray baute man seine Treppe im Studio nach. / Après la répétition dans la maison de Nicholas Ray, les escaliers sont reproduits en studio.

**STILL FROM 'REBEL WITHOUT A CAUSE'
(1955)**
When his father, who clearly supports doing the right
thing, won't speak up, Jim explodes. / Jims Vater ist
eindeutig dafür, dass Jim zur Polizei geht, aber er
schweigt wieder einmal und bringt Jim damit zur
Weißglut. / Face à la lâcheté de son père qui refuse de
le soutenir, Jim sort de ses gonds.

**STILL FROM 'REBEL WITHOUT A CAUSE'
(1955)**
Son and father share a sense of justice, but only the son
fights for it. / Vater und Sohn besitzen den gleichen
Sinn für Gerechtigkeit, doch nur der Sohn kämpft
darum. / Le père et le fils ont tous deux le sens de la
justice, mais seul Jim est prêt à se battre pour elle.

116

**STILL FROM 'REBEL WITHOUT A CAUSE'
(1955)**
Jim's red jacket is the emblem of his passionate
nature. / Jims rote Jacke symbolisiert seine
Leidenschaft. / Son blouson rouge est l'emblème de
son tempérament passionné.

*"He said it didn't matter how your lines came out
or what crazy kind of behavior you did with your
characters. He said you could do Hamlet's
soliloquy walking on your hands and eating a
carrot as long as an audience could see your eyes
and believe you, that your feelings when you are
an honest actor show through your eyes."*
Dennis Hopper

*„Er sagte, es spiele keine Rolle, wie man seinen
Text spricht oder wie verrückt man seine Rolle
anlegt. Er sagte: Du kannst Hamlets Monolog im
Handstand halten und dabei eine Möhre kauen,
solange das Publikum deine Augen sehen kann
und es dir abnimmt. Bei einem aufrichtigen
Schauspieler zeigen sich die Gefühle in den
Augen."*
Dennis Hopper

STILL FROM 'REBEL WITHOUT A CAUSE' (1955)
Buzz's pals (including Dennis Hopper, 2nd from left) fear Jim will report them as well. / Die Kumpel von Buzz (darunter Dennis Hopper, 2. von links) fürchten, dass Jim der Polizei ihre Namen verrät. / Les copains de Buzz (parmi lesquels Dennis Hopper, 2e à partir de la gauche) craignent que Jim ne les dénonce.

« Peu lui importait la façon dont on disait son texte ou les comportements bizarres qu'on prêtait à son personnage. Selon lui, on pouvait déclamer le monologue de Hamlet en marchant sur les mains ou en mangeant une carotte, du moment que le public pouvait lire la sincérité dans votre regard. Il était convaincu que chez un acteur sincère, les émotions passent par le regard. »
Dennis Hopper

**STILL FROM 'REBEL WITHOUT A CAUSE'
(1955)**
Shaken by their losses, Jim and Judy talk deeply and
authentically, and connect. / Durch ihre Verluste
erschüttert, finden Jim und Judy in tiefsinnigen
Gesprächen zueinander. / Secoués par le drame,
Jim et Judy s'épanchent et se rapprochent.

**ON THE SET OF 'REBEL WITHOUT A CAUSE'
(1955)**
Nicholas Ray lines up a shot as Jim and Judy hide from
the angry gang. / Ray bereitet eine Einstellung mit Jim
und Judy vor, die sich vor der aufgebrachten Bande
verstecken. / Nicholas Ray cadre le plan où Jim et Judy
tentent d'échapper à la fureur de la bande.

STILL FROM 'REBEL WITHOUT A CAUSE'
(1955)
The pair hide out in a deserted mansion, where they
encounter needy Plato. / Das Paar versteckt sich in
einem verlassenen Haus, wo es „Plato" trifft, der Hilfe
braucht. / Jim et Judy se cachent dans une maison
abandonnée où ils retrouvent le malheureux Platon.

STILL FROM 'REBEL WITHOUT A CAUSE'
(1955)
A very real cameraderie and intimacy evolved on the
set. / Bei den Dreharbeiten entwickelten sich echte
Kameraderie und Freundschaft. / Une camaraderie et
une intimité bien réelles voient le jour sur le tournage.

"He was not really a rebel – not in the sense that he was rejecting his parents, or saying, 'Leave me alone. I don't want to have anything to do with you.' [...] He was really saying, 'Listen to me.' 'Hear me, love me.'"
Natalie Wood

„Er war kein wirklicher Rebell – nicht in dem Sinne, dass er seine Eltern zurückwies oder sagte: ‚Lasst mich in Ruhe! Ich will mit euch nichts zu tun haben!' … Er sagte eher: ‚Hört mir zu!', ‚Hört mich, liebt mich!'"
Natalie Wood

« Il n'était pas vraiment rebelle, du moins pas dans le sens où l'on rejette ses parents en disant "Laissez-moi, je ne veux rien avoir à faire avec vous." … Ce qu'il disait en réalité, c'était "Écoutez-moi, entendez-moi, aimez-moi." »
Natalie Wood

STILL FROM 'REBEL WITHOUT A CAUSE' (1955)
The post-nuclear family – Jim and Judy become surrogate parents to Plato. / Ersatzfamilie: Jim und Judy übernehmen bei „Plato" die Elternrolle. / Famille recomposée : Jim et Judy deviennent des parents de substitution pour Platon.

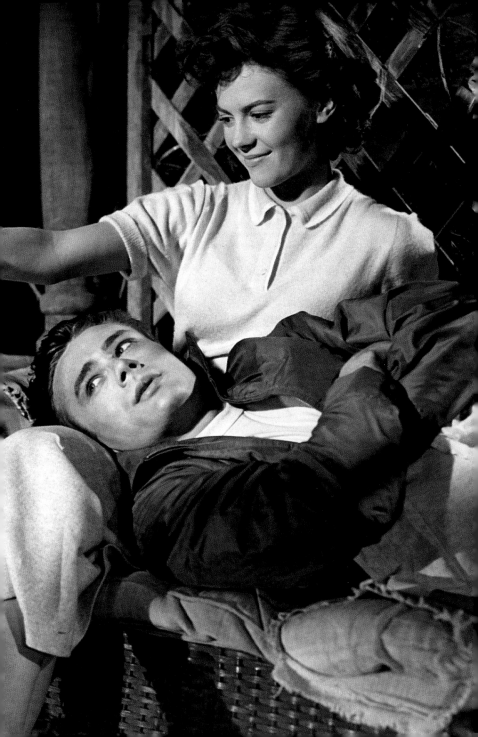

STILL FROM 'REBEL WITHOUT A CAUSE' (1955)
Judy and Jim become serious. / Es wird ernst mit Judy und Jim. / L'affaire devient sérieuse entre Judy et Jim.

PAGES 126/127
STILL FROM 'REBEL WITHOUT A CAUSE' (1955)
Jim Stark: "I've got the bullets!" His efforts to save Plato from police gunshots are tragically futile. / Jim Stark ruft: „Ich hab die Patronen!" Seine Bemühungen, „Plato" vor den Schüssen der Polizei zu retten, scheitern auf tragische Weise. / « J'ai les balles ! », s'écrie Jim dans un effort désespéré pour sauver Platon des coups de feu de la police.

ON THE SET OF 'REBEL WITHOUT A CAUSE' (1955)
Natalie Wood, out of costume, shares coffee with Dean between setups. / Natalie Wood, nicht mehr im Kostüm, gönnt sich zwischen den Einstellungen eine Tasse Kaffee mit Dean. / Natalie Wood, non costumée, boit un café avec James Dean entre deux prises.

**ON THE SET OF 'REBEL WITHOUT A CAUSE'
(1955)**
The ending was also filmed on top of the observatory.
Here the director confers with Dean. / Der Schluss
wurde ebenfalls an der Sternwarte gedreht. Hier
berät sich der Regisseur mit Dean. / Le réalisateur
s'entretient avec James Dean pendant le tournage de
la scène finale en haut de l'observatoire.

**ON THE SET OF 'REBEL WITHOUT A CAUSE'
(1955)**
Mourning the dead Plato, in the unused version of the
ending. / Eine nicht verwendete Schlussszene: Trauer
über „Platos" Tod. / Jim pleure la mort de Platon dans
une version non retenue de la scène finale.

PAGES 130 & 131
**PORTRAITS FOR 'REBEL WITHOUT A CAUSE'
(1955)**
Dean's ballet training helps him to express character
through bold physical attitude. / Deans Ballettunterricht
hilft ihm, den Charakter seiner Figuren durch Körperhaltung auszudrücken. / Sa formation de danseur
permet à Dean d'exprimer avec tout son corps le
caractère de son personnage.

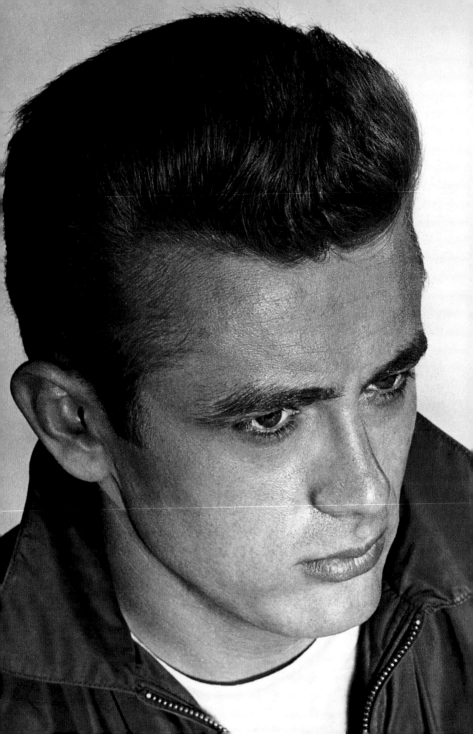

ON THE SET OF 'REBEL WITHOUT A CAUSE' (1955)

Dean was a fun guy between takes, saving his intensity for the scene itself. / Zwischen den Einstellungen war Dean immer zu Späßen aufgelegt und sparte sich seine Ernsthaftigkeit für die Kamera auf. / Gardant son intensité tragique pour le tournage, Dean fait volontiers le pitre entre les prises.

PORTRAIT FOR 'REBEL WITHOUT A CAUSE' (1955)

In character, locked and focused. / Konzentriert in seiner Rolle. / Dans la peau de son personnage, fermé et concentré.

PAGES 134/135
TRADE ADVERT FOR 'REBEL WITHOUT A CAUSE' (1955)

PAGE 136
PORTRAIT FOR 'GIANT' (1956)

James Dean plays Jett Rink, the lonely outcast turned lonely empire-builder. / James Dean spielt Jett Rink, den einsamen Außenseiter, der sich allein ein Imperium aufbaut. / James Dean dans le rôle de Jett Rink, le paria solitaire devenu un magnat tout aussi esseulé.

...and they
both come from
'good' families!

The reception committee for
the new kid on the block!

Look, ma!
No handcuffs yet!

Maybe the police s
picked up the pare

This week starts
the nationwide applause!

JAMES DEAN in
"REBEL WITHOU
A CAUSE"

WARNER BROS'. challenging drama of today's teen

CINEMASCOPE AND WARNERCOLOR

ALSO STARRING
NATALIE WOOD WITH SAL MINEO JIM BACKUS · ANN DORAN

SCREEN PLAY BY   PRODUCED BY   DIRECTED BY
COREY ALLEN · WILLIAM HOPPER · STEWART STERN · DAVID WEISBART · NICHOLAS RAY
MUSIC BY LEONARD ROSENMAN

GIANT

GIGANTEN

GÉANT

"I don't think he needed anybody or anything - except his acting."
Elizabeth Taylor

"I didn't like him. Dean was hard to be around. He hated George Stevens, didn't think he was a good director, and was always angry and full of contempt. He never smiled, was sulky and had no manners."
Rock Hudson

"Nobody had more problems with Jimmy than Jimmy. You could feel the loneliness beating out of him, and it hit you like a wave."
Mercedes McCambridge

„*Ich glaube nicht, dass er irgendjemanden oder irgendetwas brauchte - außer seiner Schauspielerei.*"
Elizabeth Taylor

„*Ich mochte ihn nicht. Es war schwierig, mit ihm zusammen zu sein. Er hasste George Stevens, hielt ihn für einen schlechten Regisseur und war immer zornig und voller Verachtung. Er lächelte nie, war mürrisch und hatte keine Manieren.*"
Rock Hudson

„*Keiner hatte größere Probleme mit Jimmy als Jimmy. Man spürte, wie die Einsamkeit aus ihm herausströmte, und sie haute einen um wie eine Welle.*"
Mercedes McCambridge

ON THE SET OF 'GIANT' (1956)
Dean meets Elizabeth Taylor on the 'Giant' set while working on 'Rebel Without A Cause.' / Dean trifft Elizabeth Taylor am Set von *Giganten*, während er noch an ... *denn sie wissen nicht, was sie tun* arbeitet. / Dean rencontre Elizabeth Taylor sur le plateau de *Géant* pendant le tournage de *La Fureur de vivre*.

PAGES 140/141
ON THE SET OF 'GIANT' (1956)
Boris Leven (right) shows his set designs to Dean and director George Stevens (left). / Boris Leven (rechts) zeigt Dean und Regisseur George Stevens (links) seine Entwürfe für das Bühnenbild. / Boris Leven (à droite) montre son projet de décor à James Dean et au réalisateur George Stevens (à gauche).

PAGES 142/143
STILL FROM 'GIANT' (1956)
An eternal man apart, Jett Rink shuns a party to stretch out in a coveted limousine. / Als ewiger Außenseiter streckt Jett Rink lieber die Beine in einer begehrten Limousine aus, als zu einer Party zu gehen. / Éternellement à l'écart, Jett Rink fuit les mondanités pour s'isoler dans une limousine convoitée.

PAGES 144/145
ON THE SET OF 'GIANT' (1956)
Whereas directors Elia Kazan and Nicholas Ray rehearsed and improvised with their actors, George Stevens was more distant, which caused tension between him and Dean. / Während die Regisseure Elia Kazan und Nicholas Ray mit ihren Darstellern probten und improvisierten, war George Stevens zurückhaltender. Das führte zu Spannungen zwischen ihm und Dean. / Alors que les réalisateurs Elia Kazan et Nicholas Ray répétaient et improvisaient avec les acteurs, George Stevens se montre plus distant, ce qui engendre des tensions avec James Dean.

« *Je pense qu'il n'avait besoin de rien ni personne, à part son métier d'acteur.* »
Elizabeth Taylor

« *Je ne l'aimais pas. Il n'était pas facile à vivre. Il détestait George Stevens, qu'il considérait comme un mauvais cinéaste, et était toujours plein de colère et de mépris. Il ne souriait jamais, il faisait la tête et était mal élevé.* »
Rock Hudson

« *Personne n'avait autant de problèmes avec Jimmy que Jimmy lui-même. On sentait la solitude qui émanait de lui et vous frappait comme une vague.* »
Mercedes McCambridge

STILL FROM 'GIANT' (1956)
Jett is, at first, a lowly cowhand smitten with his boss'
new bride, Leslie Benedict (Elizabeth Taylor). / Jett
ist anfangs ein einfacher Cowboy, der sich zu Leslie
Benedict (Elizabeth Taylor), der neuen Frau seines
Arbeitgebers, hingezogen fühlt. / Au départ, Jett est un
humble garçon de ferme amoureux de la jeune épouse
de son patron, Leslie Benedict (Elizabeth Taylor).

ON THE SET OF 'GIANT' (1956)
At first Taylor didn't know what to make of Dean, but he
won her over. / Anfangs wusste Taylor nicht so recht,
was sie von Dean halten sollte, aber schließlich konnte
er sie von sich überzeugen. / D'abord intriguée par
James Dean, Elizabeth Taylor finit par se laisser
charmer.

ON THE SET OF 'GIANT' (1956)

Dean was allowed to take photos and movie footage on set. Had he lived, he planned to direct as well as act. / Dean hatte die Erlaubnis, bei den Dreharbeiten zu fotografieren und eigene Filmaufnahmen zu machen. Neben der Schauspielerei hatte er vor, sich auch im Regiefach zu versuchen, doch dazu kam es nicht. / Autorisé à photographier et à filmer pendant le tournage, Dean ambitionne de devenir réalisateur.

PAGES 150/151
STILL FROM 'GIANT' (1956)

Jett is willed a scrap of land. "Bick" Benedict (Rock Hudson, left) and his cronies try to buy it from him. / Jett erbt ein Stück Land. „Bick" Benedict (Rock Hudson, links) und seine Kumpel versuchen, es ihm abzukaufen. / Jett hérite d'un bout de terrain, que « Bick » Benedict (Rock Hudson, à gauche) et ses acolytes tentent de lui racheter.

ON THE SET OF 'GIANT' (1956)

Dean charms Jett's creator, novelist Edna Ferber. / Auch die Autorin des Romans, Edna Ferber, erlag Deans Charme. / Dean charme l'auteur de son personnage, la romancière Edna Ferber.

"Jimmy was not only an internal actor but an expressionist, which came partly from his studying dance. He would physicalize actions, such as the way he lifted himself up on the windmill in 'Giant,' or goose-stepped measuring off the land, or his sleight-of-hand gesture as Jett Rink."
Dennis Hopper

„Jimmy war nicht nur ein Schauspieler, der in sich hineinging, sondern auch ein Expressionist, was teilweise von seinem Tanzunterricht herrührte. Er wandelte Handlungen in Körpersprache um, zum Beispiel wie er sich in Giganten auf die Windmühle schwang oder das Land abschritt, um es zu vermessen, oder seine Fingerfertigkeit als Jett Rink."
Dennis Hopper

« Jimmy ne se contentait pas d'intérioriser ses personnages, c'était aussi un expressionniste, notamment parce qu'il avait étudié la danse. Il exprimait les choses de manière physique, par exemple en grimpant sur le moulin dans Géant, ou en arpentant son bout de terrain, ou en faisant ce geste de prestidigitateur dans le rôle de Jett Rink. »
Dennis Hopper

STILL FROM 'GIANT' (1956)
Jett won't sell his tiny property – he hopes against huge odds to find oil on it. / Jett weigert sich, sein Grundstück zu verkaufen. Entgegen aller Wahrscheinlichkeit hofft er, dort Öl zu finden. / Jett refuse de vendre son terrain, espérant envers et contre tout y découvrir du pétrole.

STILL FROM 'GIANT' (1956)
Little Reata, Jett's postage stamp of a home, and hope
of wealth. / In seinem briefmarkengroßen „Little Reata"
steckt Jetts ganze Hoffnung auf künftigen Wohlstand. /
Little Reata, le terrain grand comme un mouchoir de
poche dans lequel Jett fonde tous ses espoirs.

STILL FROM 'GIANT' (1956)
An iconic, Christlike pose, down to the crossing of his
feet. / Eine ikonische, christusgleiche Pose – bis hinab
zu den übereinandergestellten Füßen. / Dans une
posture christique jusqu'à la pointe des orteils.

STILL FROM 'GIANT' (1956)
Leslie sees that Jett is improving himself with writing courses. / Leslie sieht, dass Jett an sich arbeitet und Unterricht im Schreiben nimmt. / Leslie découvre que Jett prend des cours d'écriture pour progresser.

"[Director George] Stevens has been horrible. I sat there for three days, made up and ready to work at 9 o'clock every morning. By 6 o'clock I hadn't had a scene or a rehearsal. I sat there like a bump on a log watching that hog lumpy Rock Hudson making love to Liz Taylor. I'm not going to take it anymore."
James Dean

„[Regisseur George] Stevens war schrecklich. Ich saß drei Tage lang in voller Maske um 9 Uhr morgens da und war bereit zur Arbeit. Als es 18 Uhr war, hatte ich nicht eine einzige Szene gedreht oder auch nur eine Probe gemacht. Ich saß da rum wie bestellt und nicht abgeholt und musste zusehen, wie dieses fette Schwein Rock Hudson Liz Taylor abknutschte. Ich mach das nicht länger mit."
James Dean

STILL FROM 'GIANT' (1956)
He serves her tea, a further sign of his sweetness and
refined aspirations. / Dass er ihr Tee serviert, ist ein
weiteres Zeichen für seine Bemühungen um kultivierte
Lebensart. / La façon dont il lui offre le thé trahit sa
douceur et sa soif de raffinement.

« [Le réalisateur George] Stevens a été atroce.
Je suis resté là pendant trois jours, maquillé et prêt
à bosser dès 9 heures du matin. Mais à 6 heures
du soir, je n'avais pas tourné une scène ni répété
quoi que ce soit. Je restais posé là comme un sac,
à regarder ce cochon de Rock Hudson faire l'amour
à Liz Taylor. Je ne me laisserai plus traiter comme
ça. »
James Dean

ON THE SET OF 'GIANT' (1956)
Off-camera hijinks between Dean, Taylor and Hudson echo the onscreen drama: Jett Rink is trying to lure Leslie away from "Bick." / Was sich abseits der Kamera zwischen Dean, Taylor und Hudson abspielt, spiegelt die Handlung auf der Leinwand wider: Jett Rink versucht, Leslie von „Bick" fortzulocken. / Les pitreries de Dean, Taylor et Hudson en dehors du plateau reflètent l'intrigue du film : Jett tente de détourner Leslie de « Bick ».

ON THE SET OF 'GIANT' (1956)
Locating Jett's defiant stance, investing it with his own. / Dean denkt sich in Jetts trotzige Haltung hinein und bringt seine eigene in die Rolle ein. / Dean habite le personnage de Jett en lui prêtant sa propre attitude rebelle.

STILL FROM 'GIANT' (1956)
As Leslie leaves his land, her footsteps reveal oil, giving
Jett renewed hope. / Als Leslie sein Grundstück
verlässt, bilden sich in ihren Fußstapfen Ölpfützen, die
Jett neue Hoffnung geben. / Quand Leslie repart, ses
traces de pas révèlent la présence de pétrole, donnant
à Jett un nouvel espoir.

*"James Dean was a genius. I don't think there's
another actor in the world who could've portrayed
Jett as well as he did. But, like most geniuses, Dean
suffered from success poisoning. Utterly winning
one moment, obnoxious the next."*
Edna Ferber, author of 'Giant'

„*James Dean war ein Genie. Ich glaube, es gibt
keinen anderen Schauspieler auf der Welt, der Jett
so gut dargestellt hätte wie er. Aber wie die
meisten Genies wurde Dean vom Erfolg verdorben.
Er konnte äußerst einnehmend sein und im
nächsten Augenblick einfach widerlich.*"
Edna Ferber, Autorin von *Giganten*

STILL FROM 'GIANT' (1956)
Jett's patience and lone, hard work win him our sympathy. / Mit seiner Geduld und seiner harten, einsamen Arbeit gewinnt Jett die Sympathien des Publikums. / Sa patience et son dur labeur solitaire gagnent la sympathie du public.

PAGES 162/163
STILL FROM 'GIANT' (1956)
Gusher! The long scenes of buildup make this an exhilarating moment. / Öl! In diesem berauschenden Augenblick löst sich die über lange Szenen aufgebaute Spannung. / Victoire! Les longues séquences de préparation rendent la scène particulièrement grisante.

« James Dean était un génie. Je ne crois pas qu'il y ait un seul acteur au monde qui aurait pu incarner Jett aussi bien que lui. Mais comme la plupart des génies, Dean était intoxiqué par le succès. Il pouvait être absolument charmant et devenir odieux l'instant suivant. »
Edna Ferber, auteur du roman Géant

STILL FROM 'GIANT' (1956)
Jett's psychological rebirth is both a blessing and a
curse. This scene was cut from the film. / Jetts geistige
Wiedergeburt ist sowohl ein Segen als auch ein Fluch.
Diese Szene wurde aus dem Film herausgeschnitten. /
La renaissance de Jett est à la fois une bénédiction et
une malédiction. Cette scène a été coupée au montage.

STILL FROM 'GIANT' (1956)
Driving to "Bick", and Leslie: he can't wait to share his
good news with the high and mighty Benedicts. / Jett
fährt zu „Bick" und Leslie: Er kann es kaum erwarten,
den hochnäsigen Benedicts seine gute Nachricht zu
überbringen. / En route vers le vaste ranch de son
puissant voisin « Bick » et de sa femme Leslie, auxquels
il a hâte d'annoncer la bonne nouvelle.

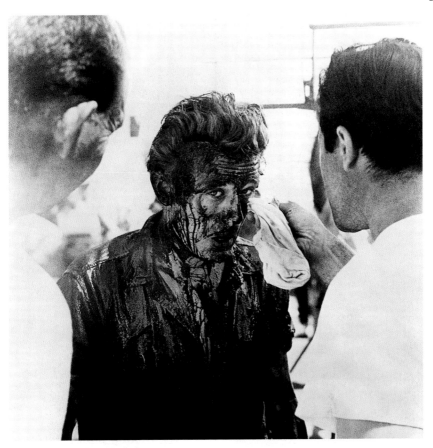

ON THE SET OF 'GIANT' (1956)
The meticulous physical detail is typical of a George Stevens production. / Genauigkeit bis ins kleinste Detail ist das Markenzeichen einer typischen George-Stevens-Produktion. / Le soin méticuleux apporté aux détails physiques est caractéristique des films de George Stevens.

STILL FROM 'GIANT' (1956)
"I'm a rich 'un", Jett brags in triumph. / Triumphierend prahlt Jett: „Ich bin reich!" / « Je suis riche », lance Jett d'un air triomphal.

STILL FROM 'GIANT' (1956)
"Bick," primally threatened, replies to Jett's amorous wisecrack. / „Bick", der sich in seiner Männlichkeit getroffen fühlt, reagiert auf Jetts amouröse Anspielung. / Menacé au plus profond de lui, « Bick » répond à la plaisanterie galante de Jett.

STILL FROM 'GIANT' (1956)
Intoxicated with his newfound wealth, Jett slyly propositions Leslie. / Von seinem plötzlichen Reichtum berauscht, macht Jett Leslie einen unsittlichen Antrag. / Grisé par sa soudaine fortune, Jett fait des avances sournoises à Leslie.

STILL FROM 'GIANT' (1956)
Jett also decks her idealistic son Jordan (Dennis Hopper) at a ceremony meant to cement Jett's reputation. / Jett verprügelt auch ihren idealistischen Sohn Jordan (Dennis Hopper) bei einer Feier, die eigentlich Jetts Reputation in der Gesellschaft festigen sollte. / Lors d'une cérémonie censée asseoir sa réputation, Jett assomme Jordan (Dennis Hopper), le fils idéaliste des Benedict.

STILL FROM 'GIANT' (1956)
Denied his ideal woman, Jett waits 20 years to woo her daughter Luz (Carroll Baker), named after the woman who willed him the oil-rich land. / Weil ihm die Frau seiner Träume versagt war, wartet Jett 20 Jahre, um ihrer Tochter Luz (Carroll Baker) den Hof zu machen, die den Namen jener Frau trägt, die ihm einst das ölreiche Land vermachte. / Privé de la femme de ses rêves, Jett attend 20 ans pour courtiser sa fille Luz (Carroll Baker), qui porte le nom de celle qui lui a légué son lopin de terre.

172

STILL FROM 'GIANT' (1956)
A smoldering lifelong rivalry erupts: "Bick" and Jett
square off. / Eine lebenslang schwelende Rivalität
kommt zum Ausbruch: „Bick" und Jett tragen ihren
Streit mit den Fäusten aus. / Laissant éclater leur vieille
rivalité larvée, « Bick » et Jett se mettent en garde.

OPPOSITE/RECHTS/CI-CONTRE
STILL FROM 'GIANT' (1956)
Fascinating to imagine how Dean would have grown old.
Jett will have to suffice. / Die Vorstellung, wie ein alter
James Dean wohl ausgesehen hätte, ist faszinierend,
doch die Welt muss mit einem gealterten Jett
vorliebnehmen. / Est-ce ainsi que James Dean aurait
vieilli ? Libre à nous de l'imaginer.

*"I think he would have surpassed both Marlon and
me. I think he really would have gone into the
classics."*
Paul Newman

*„Ich glaube, er hätte sowohl Marlon als auch mich
übertroffen. Ich denke, er wäre wirklich ein
Klassiker geworden."*
Paul Newman

*« Je pense qu'il nous aurait tous les deux surpassés,
Marlon et moi. Je crois qu'il serait entré dans les
classiques. »*
Paul Newman

ON THE SET OF 'GIANT' (1956)
Stevens choreographs the standoff between Jett and "Bick." In the end, "Bick" walks away. / Stevens choreografiert das Duell zwischen Jett und „Bick". Am Ende geht „Bick" davon. / Stevens chorégraphie la confrontation entre Jett et « Bick », qui finira par abandonner.

ON THE SET OF 'GIANT' (1956)
Stevens and Dean, both headstrong, quarreled – but to the film's benefit. / Die häufigen Auseinandersetzungen zwischen den beiden Sturköpfen Stevens und Dean kamen dem Film letztendlich zugute. / Les affrontements sont nombreux entre Stevens et Dean, deux fortes personnalités, mais le film y gagne en qualité.

STILL FROM 'GIANT' (1956)
At the time of his greatest triumph over the Benedicts,
Jett collapses dead drunk onto his speech. /
Im Augenblick seines größten Triumphs über die
Benedicts bricht Jett sturzbetrunken über seiner Rede
zusammen. / À l'heure de son plus grand triomphe sur
les Benedict, Jett s'effondre ivre mort sur son discours.

STILL FROM 'GIANT' (1956)
Later, giving his speech to an empty hall, Jett remains a
rebel against circumstance, pining for his lost love. /
Später, als er die Rede vor einem leeren Saal hält, ist
Jett noch immer ein Rebell, der den Umständen trotzt
und nach seiner verlorenen Liebe schmachtet. /
Prononçant son discours face à une salle vide, Jett
continue de se rebeller contre son sort en se
languissant de son amour perdu.

PAGES 178/179
TRADE ADVERT FOR 'GIANT' (1956)

PAGE 180
PORTRAIT FOR 'EAST OF EDEN' (1955)

GIANT

GEORGE STEVENS' PRODUCTIO

FROM THE
NOVEL BY
*EDNA
FERBER*

PRESENTED BY WARNER BROS. IN WARNERCOLOR STARRING

ELIZABETH TAYLOR · ROCK HUDSO

WITH DENNIS HOPPER · JUDITH EVELYN · PAUL FIX · SCREEN PLAY BY FRED GUIOL AND IVAN MOFFAT · MUSIC COMPOSED AND CONDUCTED BY DIMITRI

THIS IS ONE OF THE ADS IN THE SWEEPING GIANT CAMPAIGN.
APPEARS IN LIFE ON STANDS OCT. 18 AND IN LOOK ON STANDS OCT. 3

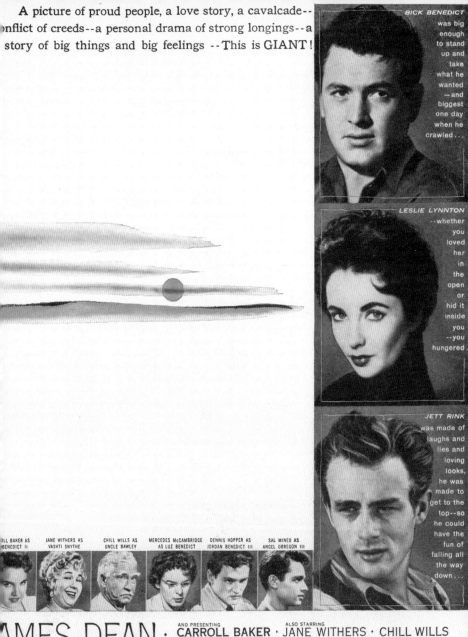

3
CHRONOLOGY

CHRONOLOGIE

CHRONOLOGIE

CHRONOLOGY

8 February 1931 James Byron Dean is born to Mildred Wilson (born 15 September 1910) and dental technician Minton Dean (born 17 January 1908) in Marion, Indiana.

1932–1936 The family of three moves four times in four years. Mildred and her son bond deeply – she is a gifted performer and storyteller, he has inherited her talent, and they share a world of active imagination together.

1937 Minton lands a job with the Veteran's Administration so the trio move to California. In addition to commencing first grade, James studies tap dancing and the violin.

14 July 1940 Mildred dies from ovarian cancer. Minton ships the boy back to Indiana alone with his mother's coffin. Although James is always civil with his father, the profound, inconsolable gap between them is lifelong.

1941–1948 James is reared on his Aunt's farm in Fairmount, Indiana. In the first months after his mother's funeral he is repeatedly found clinging to her headstone. He settles into a robust adolescence – basketball, school plays, statewide oratory competitions – and excels at them all.

1949 Graduates high school, and leaves the following week for Los Angeles. Tells his family he wants to study law but plans to become an actor.

1950 UCLA production of *Macbeth*. First professional acting assignment is dancing with other teens in a TV commercial for Pepsi-Cola.

1951 Drops out of UCLA. In April, plays John the Apostle in a live Easter broadcast, *Hill Number One*, on CBS television – girls at Immaculate Heart High School in Los Angeles immediately form the first James Dean Appreciation Society. Bit player in *Fixed Bayonets* (1951), *Sailor Beware* (1951), *Trouble Along the Way* (1951), and *Has Anybody Seen My Gal?* (1952). Moves to New York City and is a stunt-tester on TV's *Beat the Clock*.

1952–1953 Admitted into The Actors Studio. Appears in 16 television dramas, and three works

for the stage. His most commercially successful role is as Bakir, the androgynous, deceitful young manservant in André Gide's *The Immoralist*.

1954 Elia Kazan invites Dean to play the lead in his film *East of Eden*, written by John Steinbeck. Dean's star rises at meteoric speed, with offers to star in *Rebel Without a Cause*, to be directed by Nicholas Ray, and costar in *Giant*, to be directed by George Stevens. With money from *East of Eden*, Dean buys his first sports car, a used MG TA. There is more TV work, including *The Dark, Dark Hours*, as a young killer subdued by a country doctor – played by Ronald Reagan.

1955 Work with Kazan and Stevens proves turbulent, while his collaboration with Ray is happy. Relaxes by racing sports cars. In March, he buys a 1500cc Porsche super speedster and wins races in Pasadena and Pacific Palisades.

21 September 1955 Following a tip from his friend and mechanic, Rolf Wutherich, Dean trades in his Porsche speedster for the new, lighter, faster Porsche Spyder 550.

22 September 1955 Finishes filming on *Giant*.

30 September 1955, 5:45 pm James Dean is killed almost instantly in a car crash just south of Cholame, California. Donald Turnupseed fails to glimpse Dean's low-slung Spyder approaching at 65 miles per hour in the late afternoon twilight. When Turnupseed crosses against the right of way, the collision shatters the eggshell-hulled Spyder and propels it into a roadside ditch. Wutherich is thrown from the passenger seat and suffers multiple injuries. Dean is impaled on the steering column, neck broken, and dies as he is pried loose and placed on a stretcher at the scene. Turnupseed, protected by his heavy Ford sedan, is shaken but merely scratched.

PORTRAIT (1955)

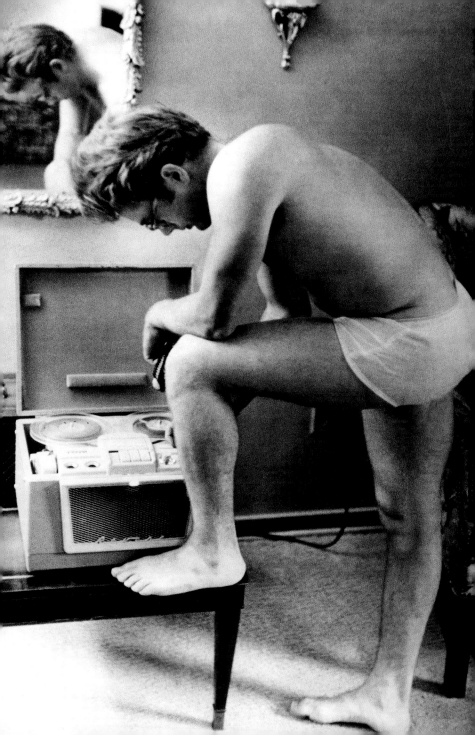

CHRONOLOGIE

8. Februar 1931 James Byron Dean wird in Marion, Indiana, geboren. Seine Eltern sind Mildred Wilson (geb. am 15. September 1910) und der Zahntechniker Minton Dean (geb. am 17. Januar 1908).

1932–1936 In vier Jahren zieht die Familie viermal um. Mildred und ihr Sohn haben eine enge Beziehung zueinander – sie ist eine begabte Erzählerin und Schauspielerin, er hat ihr Talent geerbt, und gemeinsam teilen sie eine eigene Welt der Fantasie.

1937 Weil Minton Arbeit bei der Kriegsveteranenbehörde findet, zieht die Familie nach Kalifornien. James wird eingeschult und nimmt zusätzlich Stepptanz- und Geigenunterricht.

14. Juli 1940 Mildred stirbt an Eierstockkrebs. Minton schickt den Jungen allein mit dem Sarg der Mutter nach Indiana zurück. James benimmt sich seinem Vater gegenüber zwar immer anständig, aber lebenslang bleibt eine tiefe, unversöhnliche Kluft zwischen Vater und Sohn.

1941–1948 James wächst nun auf dem Bauernhof seiner Tante in Fairmount, Indiana, auf. In den ersten Monaten nach der Beerdigung seiner Mutter wird er immer wieder gesehen, wie er sich an ihren Grabstein klammert. Doch verläuft seine Jugend später normal: Er spielt Basketball und Schultheater, nimmt an Landeswettbewerben für Rhetorik teil, und das alles mit großem Erfolg.

1949 Eine Woche nach seinem Schulabschluss an der Highschool geht er nach Los Angeles. Seiner Familie erzählt er, dass er Jura studieren möchte, doch in Wirklichkeit will er Schauspieler werden.

1950 *Macbeth*-Aufführung an der UCLA. Seinen ersten Auftritt als Berufsschauspieler hat er als Tänzer in einer Gruppe von Teenagern in einem Fernsehwerbespot für Pepsi-Cola.

1951 Er bricht das Studium an der UCLA ab. Er spielt den Apostel Johannes in einem zu Ostern live ausgestrahlten Fernsehspiel mit dem Titel *Hill Number One* auf CBS, worauf die Schülerinnen an der Highschool des Unbefleckten Herzens spontan den ersten James-Dean-Fanclub gründen. Er spielt Komparsenrollen in *Der letzte Angriff* (1951), *Seemann, paß auf!* (1951), *Ärger auf der ganzen Linie* (1951) und *Hat jemand meine Braut gesehen?* (1952). Er zieht nach

New York und wird Stunttester für die Fernsehshow *Beat the Clock*.

1952–1953 Er wird in das Actors Studio aufgenommen. Er tritt in 16 Fernsehspielen und drei Theaterstücken auf. Seinen größten kommerziellen Erfolg feiert er in der Rolle des Bakir, des hinterlistigen, androgynen Dieners in André Gides *Der Immoralist*.

1954 Elia Kazan lädt Dean ein, die Hauptrolle in seinem Film *Jenseits von Eden* nach dem Roman von John Steinbeck zu spielen. Deans rascher Aufstieg scheint unaufhaltsam, als man ihm anschließend auch noch die Hauptrolle in *... denn sie wissen nicht, was sie tun* unter der Regie von Nicholas Ray und eine der Hauptrollen in *Giganten* unter der Regie von George Stevens anbietet. Von der Gage, die er für *Jenseits von Eden* erhält, kauft sich Dean seinen ersten Sportwagen, einen gebrauchten MG TA. Er tritt auch weiter im Fernsehen auf, unter anderem in *The Dark, Dark Hours* als junger Mörder, der von einem Landarzt (Ronald Reagan) zur Strecke gebracht wird.

1955 Die Arbeit unter Kazan und Stevens erweist sich als turbulent, während die Zusammenarbeit mit Ray sehr glücklich verläuft. Zwischendurch entspannt er sich, indem er Autorennen fährt. Im März kauft er sich einen Porsche 356 Super Speedster 1500 und siegt bei Rennen in Pasadena und Pacific Palisades.

21. September 1955 Auf Rat seines Freundes, des Mechanikers Rolf Wütherich, tauscht Dean seinen Porsche Speedster gegen den neuen, leichteren und schnelleren Porsche 550 Spyder ein.

22. September 1955 Er beendet die Dreharbeiten zu *Giganten*.

30. September 1955, 17:45 Uhr James Dean stirbt bei einem Autounfall südlich von Cholame in Kalifornien. Im schrägen Licht der Abendsonne übersieht Donald Turnupseed Deans niedrigen Spyder, der sich ihm mit etwa 105 km/h nähert. Als er dessen Vorfahrt missachtet, zerschmettert der Aufprall die eierschalendünne Karosserie des Spyder und katapultiert sie in den Straßengraben. Wütherich wird vom Beifahrersitz geschleudert und schwer verletzt. Dean wird mit gebrochenem Genick von der Lenksäule aufgespießt und stirbt, als man ihn davon löst. Turnupseed, durch seine schwere Limousine geschützt, trägt nur leichte Verletzungen davon.

CHRONOLOGIE

8 février 1931 James Byron Dean naît à Marion (Indiana) de Mildred Wilson (née le 15 septembre 1910) et du technicien dentaire Minton Dean (né le 17 janvier 1908).

1932–1936 James et ses parents déménagent quatre fois en quatre ans. Profondément lié à sa mère, dont il a hérité du talent de comédienne et de conteuse, il partage avec elle son univers imaginaire.

1937 Minton ayant obtenu un poste auprès du ministère des Anciens combattants, la petite famille s'installe en Californie. Lors de son entrée à l'école primaire, James se met à étudier les claquettes et le violon.

14 juillet 1940 Mildred succombe à un cancer des ovaires. Minton renvoie son fils dans l'Indiana, seul avec le cercueil de sa mère. Bien que les rapports de James avec son père demeurent courtois, il subsistera toujours entre eux une fracture profonde et incurable.

1941–1948 James est élevé dans la ferme de sa tante à Fairmount, dans l'Indiana. Durant les premiers mois suivant le décès de sa mère, on le retrouve à plusieurs reprises agrippé à sa pierre tombale. Devenu un adolescent dynamique, il pratique le basket-ball, le théâtre et les concours d'éloquence, autant de disciplines dans lesquelles il excelle.

1949 Son baccalauréat en poche, il part la semaine suivante pour Los Angeles. Il annonce à sa famille qu'il souhaite étudier le droit, mais rêve en réalité de devenir acteur.

1950 Joue dans *Macbeth* à l'Université de Californie (UCLA). Remporte son premier cachet en dansant avec d'autres adolescents dans une publicité pour Pepsi-Cola.

1951 Quitte l'UCLA. En avril, il incarne l'apôtre Jean dans le téléfilm *Hill Number One* ; les élèves d'un lycée de jeunes filles fondent immédiatement son premier fan-club. Fait de la figuration dans *Baïonnette au canon* (1951), *La Polka des marins* (1951), *Un homme pas comme les autres* (1951) et *Qui donc a vu ma belle ?* (1952). Part pour New York, où il devient cascadeur dans le jeu télévisé *Beat the Clock*.

1952–1953 Est admis à l'Actors Studio. Apparaît dans 16 téléfilms et trois pièces de théâtre. Son plus grand succès commercial est la pièce tirée de *L'Immoraliste* d'André Gide, où il incarne un jeune serviteur androgyne et perfide.

1954 Elia Kazan lui confie le premier rôle du film *À l'est d'Éden*, écrit par John Steinbeck. Son étoile atteint le firmament à une vitesse fulgurante, puisqu'il décroche le premier rôle de *La Fureur de vivre* de Nicholas Ray et un second rôle dans *Géant* de George Stevens. Avec le cachet d'*À l'est d'Éden*, il s'achète sa première voiture de sport, une MG TA d'occasion. Il continue de tourner pour la télévision, avec notamment le téléfilm *The Dark, Dark Hours*, où il interprète un jeune assassin confronté à un médecin de campagne joué par Ronald Reagan.

1955 Le tournage avec Kazan et Stevens s'avère tourmenté, tandis que sa collaboration avec Ray est plus harmonieuse. Pour se détendre, il participe à des courses automobiles. En mars, il achète une Porsche 356 Speedster de 1500 cm3 et remporte des courses à Pasadena et Pacific Palisades.

21 septembre 1955 Sur le conseil de son ami et mécanicien Rolf Wütherich, il troque sa Porsche 356 contre une nouvelle Porsche Spyder 550, plus légère et plus rapide.

22 septembre 1955 Termine le tournage de *Géant*.

30 septembre 1955, 17h45 Près de Cholame, en Californie, James Dean est tué dans un accident de voiture. Dans la lumière du crépuscule, Donald Turnupseed ne voit pas arriver la Spyder surbaissée qui roule à 100 km/h. Lorsqu'il s'engage sur la route sans lui céder la priorité, la collision fracasse la Spyder, à la carrosserie épaisse comme une coquille d'œuf, et la propulse dans le fossé. Projeté hors du siège passager, Rolf Wütherich subit quelques blessures légères. James Dean s'empale sur la colonne de direction, la nuque brisée, et meurt tandis qu'on le désincarcère et qu'on l'étend sur une civière. Protégé par sa grosse berline Ford, Turnupseed est sous le choc, mais s'en tire avec quelques égratignures.

COVER OF 'OFFICIAL JAMES DEAN ANNIVERSARY BOOK' (1956)

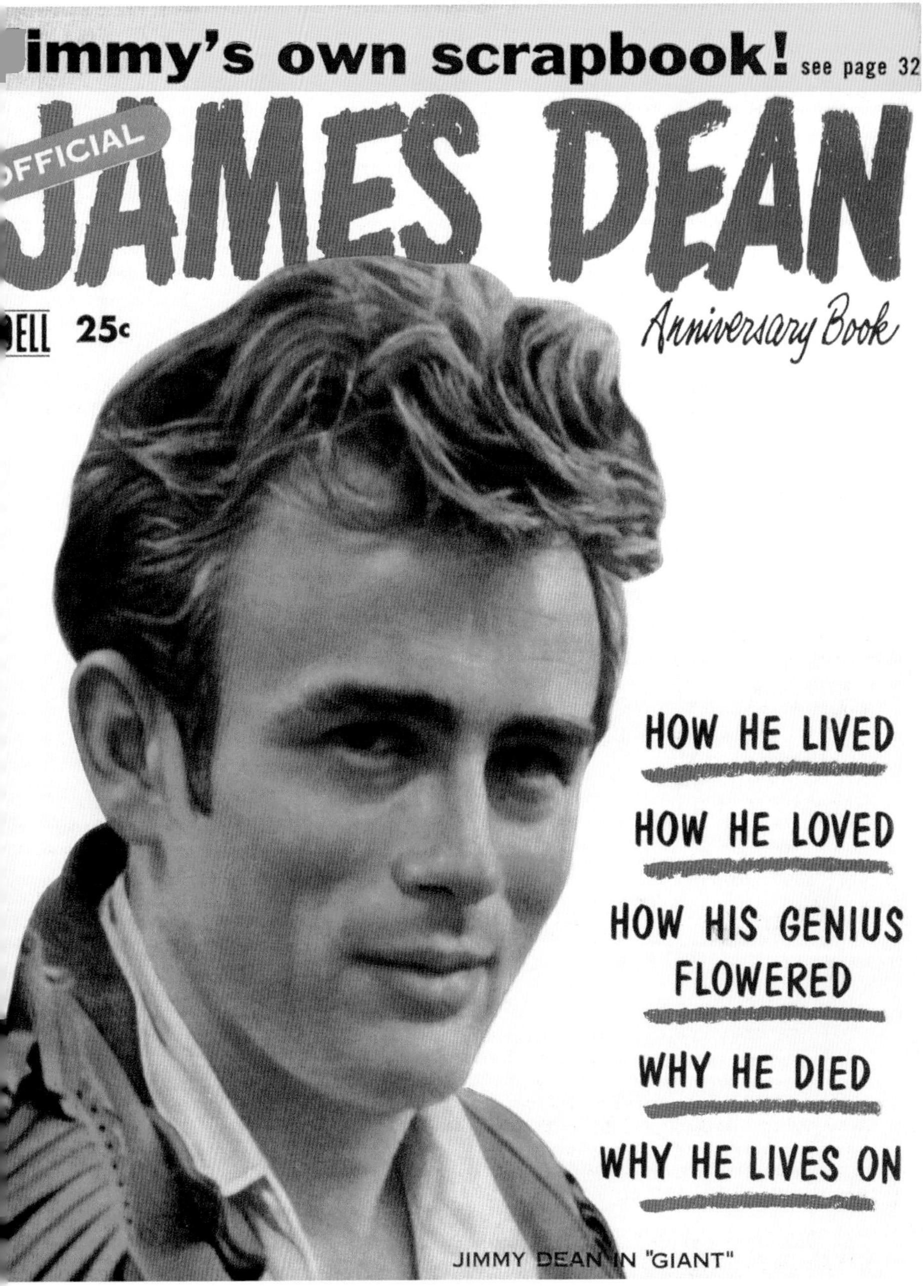

Jimmy's own scrapbook!
see page 32

OFFICIAL JAMES DEAN

Anniversary Book

DELL **25c**

HOW HE LIVED

HOW HE LOVED

HOW HIS GENIUS
FLOWERED

WHY HE DIED

WHY HE LIVES ON

JIMMY DEAN IN "GIANT"

The reception committee for the new kid on the block!

JAMES DEAN

The overnight sensation of 'East of Eden'

Warner Bros. put
all the force of
the screen
into a challenging
drama of today's
juvenile violence!

"REBEL WITHOUT A CAUSE"

IN **CinemaScope**
AND WarnerColor

...and they both come from 'good' families!

ALSO STARRING
NATALIE WOOD WITH SAL MINEO · JIM BACKUS · ANN DORAN · COREY ALLEN · WILLIAM HOPPER · STEWART STERN   MUSIC BY LEONARD ROSENMAN   PRODUCED BY DAVID WEISBART · DIRECTED BY NICHOLAS RAY   A WARNER BROS. PICTURE

4
FILMOGRAPHY

FILMOGRAFIE

FILMOGRAPHIE

"In JAMES DEAN I hail a new star. He is magnificent"

Sunday Dispatch

JOHN STEINBECK'S

EAST
OF EDEN

AN **ELIA KAZAN** PRODUCTION IN **CINEMASCOPE** WARNERCOLOR

starring **JULIE HARRIS · JAMES DEAN · RAYMOND MASSEY** with BURL IVES · RICHARD DAVALOS
JO VAN FLEET · LOIS SMITH

Screen Play by PAUL OSBORN · Directed by ELIA KAZAN

Print by TECHNICOLOR PRESENTED BY WARNER BROS.

SOON!

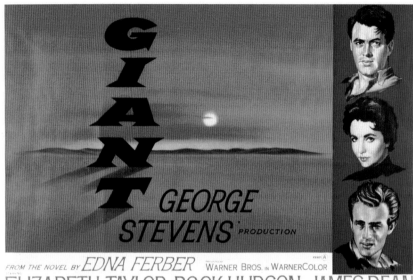

East of Eden (dt. *Jenseits von Eden,* fr. *À l'est d'Éden,* 1955)
Calvin Trask. Director: Elia Kazan.

Rebel Without a Cause (dt. *... denn sie wissen nicht, was sie tun,* fr. *La Fureur de vivre,* 1955)
James Stark. Director: Nicholas Ray.

Giant (dt. *Giganten,* fr. *Géant,* 1956)
Jett Rink. Director: George Stevens.

"James Dean was the damaged but beautiful soul of our time."
Andy Warhol

„James Dean war die beschädigte, aber schöne Seele unserer Zeit."
Andy Warhol

« James Dean était l'âme blessée mais sublime de notre époque. »
Andy Warhol

BIBLIOGRAPHY

Adams, Leith & Burns, Keith: *James Dean, Behind the Scene.* Citadel Press, 1990.

Alexander, Paul: *James Dean.* Goldmann, 2002.

Bulteau, Michel: *James Dean: un beau cadavre.* Éditions du Rocher 2005.

Dalton, David: *James Dean: The Mutant King.* Straight Arrow Books/Simon & Schuster, 1974.

Dalton, David: *James Dean, American Icon.* St. Martin's Press, 1984.

Dalton, David (Introduction), Betrock, Alan & Fagnani, Jerry (Eds.): *James Dean REVEALED! James Dean's Sexsational Lurid Afterlife from the Scandal and Movie Magazines of the 1950s.* Delta Books, 1991.

Gehring, Wes D.: *James Dean, Rebel With a Cause.* Indiana Historical Society Press, 2005.

Grant, Neil: *James Dean, In His Own Words.* Crescent Books/Random House, 1991.

Holley, Val: *James Dean, The Biography.* St. Martin's Press, 1995.

Hoskyns, Barney: *James Dean, Shooting Star.* Doubleday, 1989.

Hyams, Joe & Hyams, Jay: *James Dean, Little Boy Lost.* Warner Books, 1992.

Martinetti, Ronald: *The James Dean Story.* Birch Books/Carol, 1995.

Mayer-Stabley, Bertrand: *James Dean.* Éditions Payot, 2005.

Perry, George: *James Dean, A 50th Anniversary Tribute Authorized by the James Dean Estate.* DK Publishing/Penguin, 2005.

Reise, Randall: *James Dean, His Life and Legacy from A to Z.* Contemporary Books, 1991.

Schatt, Roy: *James Dean, A Portrait.* Delilah Books/G. P. Putnam, 1982.

Sheridan, Liz: *Dizzy & Jimmy, My Life With James Dean, A Love Story.* Reganbooks HarperCollins, 2000.

Spoto, Donald: *Rebel - The Life & Legend of James Dean.* HarperCollins, 1996.

Stock, Dennis: *James Dean Revisited.* Chronicle Books, 1986.

Tanitch, Robert: *The Unknown James Dean - Theatre, Film, Television.* BT Batsford, 1997.

IMPRINT

© 2007 TASCHEN GmbH
Hohenzollernring 53, D-50672 Köln
www.taschen.com

Editor/Picture Research/Layout: Paul Duncan/Wordsmith Solutions
Editorial Coordination: Martin Holz, Cologne
Production Coordination: Nadia Najm and Horst Neuzner, Cologne
German Translation: Thomas J. Kinne, Nauheim
French Translation: Anne Le Bot, Paris
Multilingual production: www.arnaudbriand.com, Paris
Typeface Design: Sense/Net, Andy Disl and Birgit Reber, Cologne

Printed in Italy
ISBN 978-3-8228-2220-3

To stay informed about upcoming TASCHEN titles, please request our magazine at www.taschen.com/magazine or write to TASCHEN, Hohenzollernring 53, D-50672 Cologne, Germany, contact@taschen.com, Fax: +49-221-254919. We will be happy to send you a free copy of our magazine which is filled with information about all of our books.